C000185243

Kingdom Come

Essential theology for the twenty-first century

— MARK PHILPS —

Sacristy
Press

Sacristy Press
PO Box 612, Durham, DH1 9HT

www.sacristy.co.uk

First published in 2019 by Sacristy Press, Durham

Sacristy Limited, registered in England & Wales, number 7565667

British Library Cataloguing-in-Publication Data
A catalogue record for the book is available from the British Library

ISBN 978–1–78959–003–6

For Caroline
without whom none of this would have been written

Preface

This book is about the Kingdom of God: it grew out of a conviction that treating Jesus' proclamation of the Kingdom as the foundation of our theology enables everything else to fall into place. Without that gravitational centre the New Testament doesn't hold together: bits fly off in all directions and develop an independent life of their own.

The book is intended primarily for those who have, or hope to have, a teaching ministry in the life of the church, and anybody else who is interested in the coherence and relevance of the Christian faith. My aim is to provide a framework for understanding and applying the New Testament which will enable the church's leaders and teachers to shape the life of God's people according to God's purposes.

This means that the book deals in theology (sometimes quite demanding theology) because theology matters to those who want to follow Jesus. He was a theologian, and so were Paul and the other New Testament authors.

I learned the necessity of theology in my first year of training for ordained ministry in the Church of England. I was with a small group of fellow new recruits meeting with one of the College tutors: one of us dared to question why we needed to do theology at all. We had the Bible: surely theology was not necessary? The reply came back fast and sharp: everybody has a theology—the question is whether it's any good or not. He was right. We all have a theology: we have ideas, thoughts, and images in our hearts and minds about God and his purposes (quite possibly even if we don't believe in him). Whether those thoughts and images are accurate or not is another matter. Bad theology leads to bad fruit—at least in the long run. If we believe wrong things, that will show up in the lives we lead and the faith we pass on to other people.

Theology has been much maligned. Harold Wilson dismissed disputes within the Labour Party over Clause Four as "theology", suggesting impenetrable obscurity and nitpicking irrelevance to any practical concerns. But theology *is* practical. It's practical because it's about ideas, and ideas shape nations because they shape people. During the dark days of the Soviet Union I stood in the queue at Sheremetyevo airport in Moscow, listening to the female customs officer asking each person just one question: "Do you have any books, newspapers, magazines, or Bibles?" I realized then that this supposedly mighty regime was, above all things, frightened of words, of ideas and information which might invade its territory and challenge its grip on power. Fortunately, when it came to my turn, the woman omitted to mention Bibles.

This is not a "how to" book. It will not tell you how to preach the gospel, or disciple people, or practise spiritual gifts—there are plenty of those books already available by people much better qualified to write them than I am. Nor is it in any sense comprehensive. There are many vital topics in theology about which I have nothing useful to add. I have written only about issues which I have had to think through in the course of a life spent in parish ministry, and where I think I have something fresh to say.

Not, of course, that the ideas I have written about are all my own. I studied academic theology in the 1970s and in those days academic study of the New Testament could be a dispiriting experience. The prevailing scepticism about the historical value of the Gospels was not encouraging to one about to embark on a lifetime of Christian ministry. Later, I discovered the work of Tom Wright. Here was a first-rate scholar and historian whose take on the New Testament documents came as a breath of astonishingly fresh air. Several chapters of this book are indebted to Tom's work, a debt which I have acknowledged either by direct quotation or in the endnotes. My hope is that readers who have not read Tom Wright himself will go on to do so. Many people read his books and find them both illuminating and life-giving but, because some of his ideas require the reader to re-think some treasured conceptions, they fall back into the accustomed grooves of their theology for lack of time and space to integrate the new material. Anyone looking for something to focus on for a sabbatical or period of study leave would find reading and digesting Tom Wright a very profitable project.

Finally, I want to thank those who read and commented on the manuscript: Rachel Maurice, Andrew Morsley, Caroline Philps, Nick & Georgina Philps—they are not to blame for the end product. Most of all, I want to thank my family for their love, support, and patience during many years of sharing in Christian ministry. My debt to my wife, in particular, is expressed in the dedication.

Contents

C H A P T E R   1

Kingdom

The Kingdom of God spoken of in the New Testament has been variously interpreted in the course of the last 2,000 years:

- as another way of speaking of the church, the community of Christian believers
- as an invisible spiritual realm entered into at conversion
- as a life of peace, happiness, and blessing for believers after death
- as the pursuit of justice for the poor
- even as coming to expression from time to time in a particular political or social institution such as the British National Health Service

The fuzziness and the range of interpretations available for understanding the Kingdom suggest either that the New Testament is very unclear about what the Kingdom is, or that we're not listening properly to what it says.

In fact, it shouldn't be difficult to discover the meaning of this New Testament phrase. Jesus spoke more about it than anything else. He began his ministry by announcing the arrival of the Kingdom and, during his final week in Jerusalem, told the disciples that this same proclamation would continue until the consummation of God's purposes:

> This gospel of the Kingdom will be proclaimed throughout the whole world as a testimony to all nations, and then the end will come.
>
> *Matthew 24:14*

A large proportion of his parables concern the Kingdom, the Beatitudes are focused on the Kingdom, his preaching tours focus on the Kingdom, he explains his exorcisms as signs of the Kingdom: Kingdom is his constant theme. And he dies with a notice proclaiming his kingship over his head.

Definition of the Kingdom

So what is the Kingdom? The simplest definition is found in what we know as the Lord's Prayer:

> Your kingdom come, your will be done, on earth as it is in heaven.
> *Matthew 6:10*

The Kingdom is the will of God, done on earth as it is already done in heaven. This is what we see Jesus announcing as he preaches his first sermon at the synagogue in Nazareth, taking words from Isaiah 61:

> The Spirit of the Lord is upon me, because he has anointed me to proclaim good news to the poor. He has sent me to proclaim liberty to the captives and recovering of sight to the blind, to set at liberty those who are oppressed, to proclaim the year of the Lord's favour.
> *Luke 4:18–19*

This is what Jesus enacts in his ministry. Wherever he goes, sin, sickness, hunger, poverty, injustice, the spiritual forces of evil, and even death itself, are pushed back.

More than that, Jesus promises that there will come a day when the forces which spoil human life are not merely pushed back but defeated fully and finally, never to rear their heads again. He looks forward to a "new world"[1]—literally, a "new birth" for creation, a renewal of the entire cosmos. He had told Nicodemus that he must have a new birth—be "born again"—to see the Kingdom of God. Now he tells the disciples that the universe itself must, in due time, be born again too.

This is the Kingdom of God—inaugurated in the ministry of Jesus, continued in the ministry of his followers, and consummated in the rebirth of creation. This is what disciples are told to seek, to pray for, to work for, and to hope for. It is the most glorious vision ever offered to human beings. This is what the human heart longs for: the righting of all wrongs, the overturning of all injustices, the triumph of love, joy, and peace over all that spoils human life. It is the best possible good news.

Background to Jesus' understanding of the Kingdom

Where does Jesus get this glorious vision? The terms in which he makes his initial announcement, and the ready response it generates, suggest that what he is talking about is in some way familiar to his audience:

> The time is fulfilled, and the kingdom of God is at hand; repent
> and believe in the gospel.
>
> ***Mark 1:15***

"The time is fulfilled": in other words, the thing you've all been waiting for is on its way here and now. The long period of longing for God to act on behalf of his people is over.

Jesus was tapping into a story deeply embedded in Israel's scriptures. One of the key texts is the book of Daniel, which begins as the story of a small group of faithful Israelites exiled to Babylon in the sixth century before Christ. There they learn to live out their allegiance to the one true God amidst pagan idolatry and power politics. The book includes dreams and visions of the future—dreams which Daniel (the central figure in the group of faithful Israelites) finds himself called on to interpret, and visions which he receives himself.

The first dream is given to King Nebuchadnezzar, who demands not only that somebody be found to interpret the dream but also to tell him what the dream was. This is beyond the capacities of the wise men of Babylon, but Daniel is able to deliver what the King demands. He begins by telling the King the content of his dream:

> You saw, O king, and behold, a great image. This image, mighty and of exceeding brightness, stood before you, and its appearance was frightening. The head of this image was of fine gold, its chest and arms of silver, its middle and thighs of bronze, its legs of iron, its feet partly of iron and partly of clay. As you looked, a stone was cut out by no human hand, and it struck the image on its feet of iron and clay, and broke them in pieces.
>
> *Daniel 2:31–34*

Then Daniel gives the interpretation. The dream is about four successive kingdoms, represented by the different parts of the great image, beginning with Nebuchadnezzar's kingdom, which is the head of fine gold. After his kingdom there will be three other regimes, and then, "in the days of those kings":

> . . . the God of heaven will set up a kingdom that shall never be destroyed, nor shall the kingdom be left to another people. It shall break in pieces all these kingdoms and bring them to an end, and it shall stand for ever, just as you saw that a stone was cut from a mountain by no human hand, and that it broke in pieces the iron, the bronze, the clay, the silver, and the gold . . .
>
> *Daniel 2:44–45*

Later, in Chapter 7, Daniel receives a vision of four beasts, which appear to correspond to the four kingdoms of Nebuchadnezzar's dream but giving more detail about what they will be like. And then Daniel receives another vision:

> I saw in the night visions,
> and behold, with the clouds of heaven
> there came *one like a son of man,*

and he came to the Ancient of Days
  and was presented before him.
And to him was given dominion
  and glory and *a kingdom*,
that all peoples, nations, and languages
  should serve him;
his dominion is an everlasting dominion,
  which shall not pass away,
and *his kingdom one*
  that shall not be destroyed.

Daniel 7:13–14 (my italics)

When Jesus went through Palestine proclaiming the Kingdom of God and referring to himself as "the Son of Man", it would be these scriptural references which would immediately spring to mind for his hearers. They would naturally understand that he was announcing the much anticipated but long-delayed Kingdom of God prophesied by Daniel.

The good news of the Kingdom

Jesus says that the Kingdom is gospel: good news. In this he is drawing on another scriptural source—the book of Isaiah:

How beautiful upon the mountains
  are the feet of him who brings good news,
who publishes peace, who brings good news of happiness,
  who publishes salvation,
  who says to Zion, "Your God reigns."

Isaiah 52:7

The promised reign of God will launch a gospel of peace, happiness, and salvation.

The gospel is specifically good news for the poor, as Jesus' choice of Isaiah 61 for his text at the synagogue in Nazareth makes clear. In Luke's Gospel Jesus proclaims blessing particularly on the "poor" (as opposed to the "poor in spirit" in Matthew's version). Jesus' healing ministry meets the needs of the poor above all—anyone who has worked with the poor knows that ill health is more prevalent and death comes earlier in deprived areas. Of the three occasions when Jesus is recorded as raising the dead, at least one such is rooted in his concern for the poor: a widowed mother who will probably be left destitute without a son to look after her. When Jesus ministers to the rich it is often with a view to blessing the poor: the rich young ruler is told to sell his goods and give to the poor as the preliminary to becoming a disciple; after his conversation with Jesus, Zacchaeus precipitates a minor economic revolution in Jericho by publicly undertaking to give half his wealth to the poor and paying back fourfold anyone he has defrauded.

Jesus' teaching has some sharp things to say about riches. The parable of the rich man and Lazarus is a stark warning to the rich not to neglect the poor, and significantly it is the poor man who gets a name while the rich man remains anonymous. The rich man who decides to tear down his barns and build bigger ones is vividly portrayed as a fool—he does not know (or does not care) what God expects of those who have wealth. Those who "devour widows' houses"[2] are warned to expect severe condemnation. Jesus' concern for the poor echoes through the rest of the New Testament; it seems to have had a particular impact on his brother James, whose letter[3] is full of warnings to the rich and commendations of the poor. Justice for the poor is at the heart of the good news of the Kingdom.

The gospel according to Rome

The background to Jesus' life was, of course, not only the nation of Israel with its scriptures, its hopes, and its struggles, but crucially the Roman Empire. And the Empire had its own kind of "gospel". The Roman version of gospel is exemplified in a decree issued around 9 BC marking the birthday of Caesar Augustus (23 September) as the beginning of the civil year:

> Whereas the Providence (*pronoia*) which has ordered the whole of our life, showing concern and zeal, has ordained the most perfect consummation for human life by giving to it Augustus, by filling him with virtue for doing the work of a benefactor among men, and by sending in him, as it were, a saviour for us and those who come after us, to make war to cease, to create order everywhere . . . and whereas the birthday of the God [Augustus] was the beginning for the world of the gospel that has come to men through him . . . Paulus Fabius Maximus, the proconsul of the province . . . has devised a way of honouring Augustus hitherto unknown to the Greeks, which is, that the reckoning of time for the course of human life should begin with his birth.[4]

This is Rome's good news: a Saviour Emperor who has come to end war and create order, a benefactor who is filled with virtue, a god whose birthday is the beginning of the gospel and which should therefore be celebrated by making it the basis for recording the passage of time itself. This document (or at least the political and social culture which lie behind it) would have been part of the mental furniture of everybody in Palestine in the time of Jesus, and particularly so when the gospel spread out beyond their home country into the wider Empire.

Kingdoms in conflict

Jesus' gospel of the Kingdom is going to bring him and his followers into conflict with Rome's gospel. They can't both be true. Either Jesus is Lord and Saviour or Caesar is. In the long run, one or other "gospel" is going to be vindicated and the other is going to be defeated. And the conflict will not only be with Rome but with all other powers which set themselves up as the answer to the problems of human life. The conflict will not be resolved by violence. The Kingdom of God doesn't work like that. It works only through a different kind of power which comes from the Holy Spirit and is backed up by a willingness to suffer, as demonstrated in the example of Jesus himself. The Kingdom can only continue to go forward through the same power backed up by the same willingness to pay the price. John makes this clear when he writes to the churches of Asia:

> I, John, your brother and partner in the tribulation and the kingdom and the patient endurance that are in Jesus, was on the island called Patmos on account of the word of God and the testimony of Jesus.
>
> *Revelation 1:9*

Suffering ("tribulation") and Kingdom belong together. Jesus called his followers to take up their cross daily. Paul told the church in Rome that suffering has an indispensable role in the development of Christian character and is a requirement for final glorification with Christ:

> . . . we rejoice in our sufferings, knowing that suffering produces endurance, and endurance produces character, and character produces hope.
>
> *Romans 5:3–4*

> The Spirit himself bears witness with our spirit that we are children of God, and if children, then heirs—heirs of God and fellow heirs with Christ, provided we suffer with him in order that we may also be glorified with him.
>
> *Romans 8:16–17*

Responding to the gospel

Rome's gospel was proclaimed—broadcast by heralds—across the Empire. It was news which people were expected to take notice of and adjust their lives accordingly. The same is true of the gospel of the Kingdom. The apostles saw themselves as heralds proclaiming good news: not from the Emperor, who was an impostor, but from the true God, the real Saviour, the actual benefactor of humanity.

The gospel is news—momentous news about the way things are. It announces the fact of God's intervention in the world and his plans for us and for it. As such it requires a response. The response is described as "repentance":

> The time is fulfilled, and the kingdom of God is at hand; repent and believe in the gospel.
>
> ***Mark 1:15***

Repentance is popularly supposed to be an emotional response to discovering one's own sinfulness: a question of tears and anguish of heart. That may well be true at various stages in the experience of discipleship. But it is not the fundamental issue. The root of repentance is a change of mind—that is what the word means. It is the realization that, in the light of this good news of the Kingdom, I need to rethink my life. I discover that I have been going in the wrong direction and pursuing the wrong goals, and I need to stop and turn round.

Made in the image of God

There is one further dimension to Jesus' Kingdom proclamation which it is essential to be aware of. The first mention in the Hebrew Bible of the call to exercise rule or dominion is in Genesis 1, and it refers not to the rule of God but to the rule of humans:

Then God said, "Let us make humankind in our image, according
to our likeness; and let them have dominion over the fish of the
sea, and over the birds of the air, and over the cattle, and over all
the wild animals of the earth, and over every creeping thing that
creeps upon the earth."
So God created humankind in his image,
> in the image of God he created them;
> male and female he created them.
God blessed them, and God said to them, "Be fruitful and
multiply, and fill the earth and subdue it; and have dominion over
the fish of the sea and over the birds of the air and over every
living thing that moves upon the earth."

Genesis 1:26–28 (NRSV)

God's creation project was always intended to be shared with those made
in his image. Much ink has been spilt down the Christian centuries over
the meaning of "the image of God", but the obvious interpretation of the
phrase—which is evident from the way it is sandwiched between the two
parts of the command to have dominion—is that the immediate context
defines the meaning: it is the call and the capacity to exercise rule over
the earth. It is this which sets humanity apart from all the other creatures
on the planet.

In his 2017 Lent Book, *Dethroning Mammon*,[5] Justin Welby describes
his discovery that the throne of the Archbishop in Canterbury Cathedral
was too big for him—large enough to accommodate two people. He
wondered if previous incumbents had been particularly bulky characters.
He asked about this and was told that in bygone ages kings gave honour
to those they wanted to honour by inviting them to share the throne.
God's purpose is to honour those who are made in his image by sharing
his rule with them.

Sadly, Genesis 1 is soon followed by Genesis 3, which explains that
humanity's ability to rule with justice and kindness was severely damaged
through sin (so it should be no surprise that we make such a bad job of it).
But God has not abandoned his plan: the project of salvation, of restoring
his creation, is focused on getting the planned partnership with human
beings back on track. That is the point of the whole story. Creation—as

Paul will make clear in Romans 8—can only be put right when humans come into their own and are fully restored to what they were meant to be. When that great consummation arrives, the whole project can go forward unhindered by even the possibility of sin coming in to mess things up.

The Kingdom in the theology of Paul

When we come to Paul, we find that the Kingdom theme is an essential part of his theology—not as prominent as in the Gospels, but the assumed backdrop to his life and work.

At the end of the book of Acts, Luke pictures Paul under house arrest in Rome, "proclaiming the Kingdom of God and teaching about the Lord Jesus Christ with all boldness and without hindrance".[6] In Luke's mind, the Kingdom theme played a key role in Paul's proclamation of the gospel. And the Kingdom is still a significant theme in Paul's own writings—the word crops up fourteen times in his letters. That's not a huge number, particularly when you compare it with "gospel" which features some sixty-nine times. But the way he refers to Kingdom suggests that it was something he took for granted his readers would understand. They knew about Kingdom already from his (or other people's) original proclamation of the gospel.

One passage is worth looking at in some detail. Here is Paul in the climactic Chapter 15 of his first letter to the church in Corinth:

> For as in Adam all die, so also in Christ shall all be made alive. But each in his own order: Christ the firstfruits, then at his coming those who belong to Christ. Then comes the end, when he delivers the kingdom to God the Father after destroying every rule and every authority and power. For he must reign until he has put all his enemies under his feet.
>
> *1 Corinthians 15:22-25*

When "the End" comes (that is, the consummation of the New Creation when heaven and earth are renewed and brought back into full and unhindered communication with each other), Jesus will hand over the Kingdom to the Father. That means, of course, that in the meantime Paul understands him to be ruling over his Kingdom, which is exactly what he says in the last sentence of the passage quoted. Kingdom has not faded from Paul's mind or been replaced by some other theme: ruling (exercising his Kingdom) is what Jesus is currently doing. To say "Jesus is Lord"—which according to Paul is the basic Christian confession[7]—is another way of saying that he is the King.

The Kingdom is no less important to Paul's conception of the achievement of Jesus than it was to Jesus himself. He doesn't always use Kingdom language, but the central role played by that language in 1 Corinthians 15 is indicative of its importance in Paul's mind.

We have seen that the Kingdom theme is not just about God but crucially about humans too. As those who are made in the image of God, it is our calling to be involved in his rule over creation. That understanding is equally important to Paul. In Romans 5 he explains how the Messiah has undone the consequences of Adam's sin and brought the free gift of grace, righteousness, and life to humans:

> For if, because of one man's trespass, death reigned through that one man, much more will those who receive the abundance of grace and the free gift of righteousness *reign in life* through the one man Jesus Christ.
>
> **Romans 5:17 (my italics)**

The outcome of Jesus' achievement—the thing to celebrate and look forward to—is reigning in life. ("Reign" and "Kingdom" are obviously closely related concepts in any language, but in Greek the connection is even more obvious because they share the same basic root.) Because of Jesus, humanity's rule is going to be restored. In Romans 8 he goes on to develop the theme much more fully. The creation, he says, was subjected to futility and decay. But the time is coming when God's children will enter into their glorious inheritance of ruling over creation once again, and then creation will be set free from frustration and futility forever:

... the creation itself will be set free from its bondage to
corruption and obtain the freedom of the glory of the children
of God.

Romans 8:21

Paul doesn't use Kingdom language at this point, but the language of
"glory" echoes the words of Psalm 8, where "glory" is closely related to
"dominion":

... you have made him a little lower than the heavenly beings
  and crowned him with glory and honour.
You have given him dominion over the works of your hands;
  you have put all things under his feet.

Psalm 8:5–6

Both Jesus and Paul are telling a story—the same story. Jesus proclaims,
"The time is fulfilled" (Mark 1:15), which is echoed in Paul's words to
the Galatians:

... when the fullness of time had come, God sent forth his Son.

Galatians 4:4

The fullness of time to which both Jesus and Paul refer looks back to
the whole story of the Old Testament. God has been preparing for this
moment, in the call of Abraham and the story of Israel, for a long time.
This is the last act of the divine drama, when all the themes and threads
in the previous acts are brought together and finally resolved.

Reflections on the Kingdom

I want now to offer six reflections on the significance of putting the
Kingdom at the heart of our theology.

1. The story

The gospel of the Kingdom is a story. Not, of course, a work of fiction, but a narrative—a history of God's dealings with the world and his future plans for it. The Bible itself is a narrative—a "brief history of time", to borrow the title of Stephen Hawking's book. The difference is that, unlike most history, this one tells us not only where the narrative has come from but where it is going, how it will end, and how to conform one's life accordingly.

This is of enormous importance, and is often sadly forgotten or neglected by preachers and teachers, and therefore features only marginally in the consciousness of many believers. Story matters among other things because stories are what grab people's hearts and minds. Not many people are interested in theological schemes or theories, but all of us respond to stories. Stories invite us *in*, drawing us to identify with the characters and with their longing for the triumph of love, truth, and justice. This story of the Kingdom invites us in quite explicitly. That is what Jesus is doing when he comes on the scene in Galilee announcing, "The Kingdom of God is at hand." He is saying, "Forget your petty little self-focused stories which will come to nothing—get involved in the real thing."

Most people are looking for a story to get involved in. That, surely, is the power of TV soap operas, which involve people so deeply that they confuse the actors with the characters they play, and berate the ones behaving badly if they meet them in the street. More than that, it is the power of story which is at the heart of the appeal of many of the world's great religions and belief systems. Marxism is a story: a story about the onward march of history and of revolution as the route by which justice will finally be established. The Western belief in Progress, linked as it is with the theory of Evolution, is a story: it looks forward to ever-increasing levels of prosperity and well-being (though that story has become less believable and people are looking for other stories).

Stories create identity. Humans need a story to identify with and be part of, whether it's the story of a religious tradition, a nation, a tribe, a political party, an institution, a profession, a football team, or a family. The story we choose to belong to will shape our lives. God holds out to us the privilege of being written into the script of *his* story and of allowing our sense of identity to be moulded by his story.

The church has by far the best story to tell, which outplays all the others because it is the only one which has a divine guarantee attached: the resurrection of Jesus Christ from the dead. The other stories are all merely dreams, faint apprehensions of the true story, attempts to substitute human effort for what can only be achieved by the action of God himself.

2. The poor

The Protestant church too often suffers from a split personality: split between those who emphasize personal salvation and those who emphasize social justice. It should not—and need not—be so. Jesus emphasized both, and those of his followers who have achieved most have often been the ones who held fast to both justice and salvation. William Wilberforce cared deeply both about justice for the poor and the salvation of his friends. Among the heroes of faith listed by the writer to the Hebrews are those who "enforced justice".[8]

All this goes back ultimately to the pattern set by the Old Testament. The Torah legislation was designed to enable Israel to live under the rule of God and to exercise their ministry as "a kingdom of priests and a holy nation".[9] They were to reflect back to God and outwards to the wider world the divine design for human flourishing; in particular, there was much legislation to restrain the rich from getting ever richer and the poor from getting poorer. The Jubilee provision of Leviticus 25 required that every fifty years all property should revert to its ancestral ownership (though it appears that the legislation was rarely if ever adhered to). When Ahab decides he wants his neighbour Naboth's vineyard for a vegetable garden, Naboth responds indignantly: "The LORD forbid that I should give you the inheritance of my fathers."[10] And when, as a result of Jezebel's arranging for Naboth to be murdered, Ahab gains possession of the vineyard, the LORD sends Elijah to pronounce judgement on him: "In the place where dogs licked up the blood of Naboth shall dogs lick your own blood."[11]

Deuteronomy poignantly expresses the Old Testament dream that "there will be no poor among you . . . in the land that the LORD your God is giving you,"[12] and then, three verses later, acknowledges the possibility that the dream will not be fully realized and directs the proper response when that happens: "If among you, one of your brothers should become poor, in any of your towns within your land that the LORD your God is giving you, you shall not harden your heart . . . against your poor brother."

The Old Testament legislation was intended to prefigure what the Kingdom of God looked like. When Jesus arrived in Galilee proclaiming that the Kingdom was at hand, the disciples could hardly doubt that justice for the poor would be high on the agenda. His teaching and actions would confirm that at every turn. If we put Jesus' Kingdom proclamation at the heart of our theology, then justice for the poor is a non-negotiable commitment.

3. Jesus the theologian

Taking Jesus' theme of the Kingdom of God as central gives us a fresh perspective on him: it puts him firmly in the frame as a theologian. It acknowledges that Jesus had thought deeply and meditated long on the scriptures of his people and arrived at an original, radical, and clearly articulated vision of his own vocation, the vocation of Israel and of the over-arching purpose of God for the world.

For a long time the world of scholarship never quite recovered from the nineteenth-century idea that Paul had corrupted the simple gospel preached by Jesus and made it into a complicated theological system. I want to suggest that the influence runs all the other way: Paul was captivated by Jesus, including Jesus' vision of the Kingdom, and gave his life for him and his gospel. On any view Paul is one of the great intellects of antiquity. The letter to the Romans is an astonishing intellectual achievement. That such a great intellect was induced to change the direction of his life in the radical way experienced by Paul says much for the power of Jesus as thinker and theologian.

The Protestant Reformers of the sixteenth century latched on to justification by faith as the key to their theology, and in so doing put the

Pauline letters at the centre of their thinking and pushed the Gospels to the edge of the picture. The Gospels were further marginalized by upwards of one hundred and fifty years of sceptical scholarship in the nineteenth and twentieth centuries, which left very little confidence that the New Testament offered any reliable information about Jesus. As long as that consensus dominated academic discussion it was rare for anybody even to suggest the possibility that Jesus might be a serious thinker in his own right.

But if he is not a serious thinker, how seriously should we take him? Why should we entrust our lives to one whose thinking is less distinguished than the great thinkers of human history and culture?

Fortunately, a fresh wave of writing in the closing decades of the twentieth century and into the twenty-first, in which Tom Wright is a leading figure, has gone a long way to setting the record straight and re-establishing the integrity, reliability, and cogency of the New Testament witness to Jesus.

4. Human dominion [1]

We have seen that the Kingdom is not only about restoring the rule of God over his creation, but crucially about restoring the proper dominion of humanity over the created order as well. This is controversial, to say the least. I recently heard a speaker at a public meeting blame the Christian doctrine of creation for the environmental problems of the planet. It is a commonly expressed point of view. The Genesis commission to exercise dominion over the earth—so the argument goes—has given a licence to humans to exploit the planet, plunder its resources, upset ecosystems, and severely damage the heritage we leave to subsequent generations.

There is some truth in the charge. There are Christians who talk as if this is what God had in mind—as if we should get what we can out of the planet and hang the consequences. But there is no excuse for that kind of thinking. Genesis 1 is followed by Genesis 2 which speaks clearly of creation as a garden given to humans "to work it and *take care of it*" (my italics).[13] And Genesis 2 is followed by Genesis 3 which explains how humans forfeited their right relationship with creation through sin, which would suggest we need to be careful how we handle the divine commission. What was designed to flow naturally from us now needs to be monitored and frequently restrained and corrected. The Genesis account of the divine commission to rule over creation is altogether more subtle and nuanced than the critics allow or careless Christians realize.

But the charge against Genesis doesn't really stand up to serious examination. It is not the divine commission which is responsible for human damage to the planet: it is sin—humans who are out of harmony with their Creator and doing their own thing. It is simply not true that if you take away from humans the consciousness of God-given dominion over creation, all will be well and nature will flourish again. State-sponsored atheism in the former Soviet Union far outstripped the post-Christian, capitalist West in wreaking destruction on the environment.[14] Human dominion over creation is a fact: *Homo sapiens* has powers for both good and ill which exceed anything possessed by any other inhabitant of our planet. This is not "speciesism", just common-sense realism (as well as good theology). The answer to the abuse of our powers is not to deny them but to use them properly. The gospel of the Kingdom promises us that one day that dream will be fully realized.

I am fortunate enough to live in an Area of Outstanding Natural Beauty, as defined by the Countryside and Rights of Way Act 2000. What does "natural beauty" mean? In this case, it means fields wrested from the forest by our ancestors, hedges planted and carefully maintained, crops sown to provide food, animals domesticated over the course of millennia to serve human needs, woodland managed to enable a diversity of trees to flourish, human habitation planned and built to avoid ugliness . . . The beauty is not really natural at all: it is quite artificial, at least in the sense that without human intervention the landscape as we know it would disappear. Given time and opportunity, the forest would re-assert itself and take over entirely. Properly exercised, human dominion over creation is a blessing, not a curse: it enhances the natural beauty of creation, as the Lord of Creation always intended it should.

5. Human dominion [2]

Human dominion over creation has wider implications than the questions of ecology and the environment. The fact that we are made in the image of God is the presupposition and foundation of our imitation of Christ. Jesus demonstrated authority over sickness, scarcity, bad weather, demons, death, and even the Sea of Galilee. In Chapter 4 we will see how Jesus not only did all these things but encouraged his disciples to imitate him, and finally commissioned them to make more disciples who would continue in the same vein. This was not a novelty introduced by him merely to support the spread of the gospel—a temporary provision for some supernatural fireworks to induce people to believe. It was, and is, the restoration of the originally intended relationship between humans and creation.

When I first attempted to introduce this idea in a parish group dedicated to developing the ministry of healing, one of those present exclaimed indignantly, "But that's playing God!" Well yes, being made in the image of God does imply that we are designed to do some of the things He does. That will be part of what it's like to enjoy the new creation, of which more in Chapter 8. And since (according to Jesus) the Kingdom is at hand *now, now* is the appropriate time to begin the learning process. Not that I have ever walked on water or particularly expect to do so this side of the resurrection. But extraordinary things do happen at the hands of Christian believers, particularly when the need is great, the church is under pressure, or the gospel is making inroads into fresh territory.

My friend Mark Aldridge was invited to minister in Nizhnevartovsk, in a remote part of Siberia. He was met at the airport by the local pastor, Vasili. Russians can be very direct by the standards of the reticent British, so Vasili lost very little time in getting to what he wanted to talk about. The conversation went something like this:

> **Vasili:** How many people have you raised from the dead?
> **Mark:** None, I'm afraid. How about you? How
>   many have you raised from the dead?
> **Vasili:** Only five.

To us that sounds outrageous: outrageously boastful and outrageously unlikely. And by our standards it is outrageous. But our standards are not the only standards there are. Jesus told the apostles to raise the dead and at the end of his ministry instructed them to go on making disciples who would obey all that he had commanded them. It would be difficult to test the truth of this pastor's claims, but the church in Siberia is at the frontiers of the Kingdom and is likely to face opposition and even persecution in today's Russia, so why should they not experience the power of the Kingdom in raising the dead?

> "Why is it thought incredible by any of you that God raises the dead?"
>
> *Acts 26:8*

6. Christian hope

Finally, the Kingdom challenges nearly all of us with an almost forgotten and certainly much neglected dimension of Christian hope: namely, that one day God is going to renew the whole creation. The point of the whole thing—the journey's destination—is not heaven, but heaven come to earth. Until the resurrection, Christian believers will find themselves in heaven after death, much as the penitent thief was reassured by Jesus: "Today you will be with me in paradise."[15] But that's not the end of the story, which is resurrection: heaven come down to earth and the renewal of the entire cosmos.

Much of the church has lost its grip on the hope which flows from the resurrection of Jesus, so that we are left with the cartoonist's view of our future destiny: sitting on a cloud playing a harp. But it's only the cartoonist's view because it isn't far from what the church has preached for many centuries. It's a huge mistake. God is not planning to abandon this world as a failed project. The separation from which the whole creation has been suffering since the serpent got into the Garden is going to be healed: heaven and earth are coming back together again. In the rest of this book this understanding of our hope will never be far below the surface of the argument.

CHAPTER 2

Covenant

A word of warning at the outset: this chapter is probably the most demanding of the whole book. It involves some complex ideas and some detailed exploration of some of the trickiest passages in the New Testament. I suggest that anybody who finds the going too tough should skip to the following chapter and maybe give this one another go when they're feeling stronger!

We began in the last chapter to explore Jesus' theology of the Kingdom of God, suggesting that it is this which underlies and gives coherence to the entire theological system of the New Testament, including that of the apostle Paul.

The righteousness of God

Paul does, of course, have his own special emphases which arise particularly from his commission to be the apostle to the Gentiles, taking the gospel beyond its Jewish origins to the wider world, with all the conflicts and complications which that commission entailed.

One of these special emphases is the righteousness of God, which Paul announces as the theme of his letter to the Romans (Romans 1:17).

What Paul meant by "the righteousness of God" has often been a battleground: it was so at the time of the Reformation and it has become a battleground again in recent scholarship. Since it is the stated theme of his most substantial letter, it is important to understand what the battle is about and to come to a decision about which side wins the argument. If we don't get this right we will largely fail to understand not only the letter to the Romans but Galatians as well, and more besides.

There are, in essence, two views of what Paul meant by the righteousness of God.

The traditional Protestant understanding

The traditional Protestant view is that the righteousness of God is God's gift to those who believe the gospel. On this understanding, sinners who put their faith in Jesus Christ receive the righteousness of God in exchange for their sin. God gives to sinners what they do not have in themselves: his own righteousness, credited to their account.

I have in my possession a small booklet written by a well-known evangelist. It is designed to give to people at Christmas if they want to know more about Christian faith. The writer takes us in imagination to the living room of heaven on Christmas Day. There is an exchange of gifts, during which the Son presents to the Father his life of perfect righteousness lived on earth. The Father is delighted. The question then arises: What shall I (the reader) give to God? It quickly becomes embarrassingly and distressingly clear that I have no appropriate or worthy gift to offer. But seeing that I am about to leave the room in shame and disappointment, the Son steps forward and offers to include me in his gift to the Father. I have no righteousness of my own to offer, so the Son will give me his.

This is an imaginative illustration of the traditional Protestant doctrine of the righteousness of God. On this view, Paul's doctrine of the righteousness of God is about the mechanism whereby God puts sinful humans in right relationship to himself. Essentially the picture is of an exchange whereby Jesus takes my sin and gives me his righteousness instead. Through his life of perfect obedience to the Father, he has acquired what is sometimes referred to as a "treasury of merit" from which he dispenses righteousness to those who come to him in faith. His righteousness is "imputed" to them. Thus the doctrine is known as the doctrine of "imputed righteousness".

That is one view. It is widely believed today, and is supported by the *New International Version*'s original translation of Paul's Greek phrase as "*a* righteousness *from* God".[16] This, if correct, would strongly suggest that the traditional Protestant understanding of Paul's words is right: the righteousness in question is something which comes from God to humans.

The righteousness of God: a fresh perspective

The other understanding of Paul's meaning has been put forward by scholars in recent decades. On this view, the righteousness of God is not a substance or a status which God transfers to believers. It is God's righteous conduct: God doing what is right, being true to his character and his promises. It is not primarily about us at all: it is about him.

For years I accepted the traditional Protestant view uncritically and lived with it quite happily. But once I took the time to explore what some scholars (Tom Wright, in particular) have been saying in recent decades about a different understanding of Paul, I came to see that the traditional view has some serious problems, and that what is sometimes called the New Perspective (of which there are several varieties) makes a strong case.

There are several strands to the case for reading the righteousness of God as his own righteous conduct.

The law court setting

In the first place, it makes better sense of the law court setting which (as nearly all agree) is the background to language about righteousness. "Imputed righteousness" holds that the divine judge imputes his righteousness to the accused and thus acquits him. But that would be a very odd thing for a judge to do. In order to be righteous the judge must conduct the case in accordance with truth and justice: he cannot simply credit his own righteousness to the defendant without being open to a serious charge of *in*justice/*un*righteousness.

It is possible for the sinner to be pronounced "righteous" in the present time because justification brings forward the divine verdict from the future into the present, and that verdict is based on the whole life, a life which has been re-oriented towards faith in God and in which the sins and failures have been covered by the sacrifice of the cross.[17] The key factors are the achievement of the cross and the believer's incorporation into Christ.

"Imputed righteousness" sits very uncomfortably within the law court framework. That is not the way courts operate and that is not what God is doing.

Making sense of Romans 3

Secondly, understanding the righteousness of God as his own righteous conduct makes sense of the central passage in Romans 3, where Paul is explaining how God has put forth Jesus as the means of atonement for sins, an atonement which is to be received by faith:

> . . . This was to show God's righteousness, because in his divine forbearance he had passed over former sins. It was to show his righteousness at the present time, so that he might be just and the justifier of the one who has faith in Jesus.
>
> ***Romans 3:25–26***

In this context it seems fairly obvious that Paul is telling us that God is demonstrating that he has done the right thing. He has shown himself to be righteous.

The confusion arises because Paul is telling us that the death of Jesus for sins enables God to achieve *two* things, which are very closely related but not exactly the same: he is able to be just/righteous in himself *and* he is able to justify those who put their faith in Jesus.

At this point two clarifications are necessary.

The problems of English translation

Firstly, there is a problem with the English language which makes it very difficult to produce a translation of this passage which fully captures Paul's meaning. In the original Greek the words for "righteousness", "just", and "justifier" are all from the same root and their close relationship to each other is obvious. In English we can only make that point either by translating very awkwardly along these lines:

> . . . It was to show his *righteousness* at the present time, so that he
> might be *righteous* and the one who declares *righteous* the one
> who has faith in Jesus . . .

or by inventing an English verb such as "to righteous" or, as some have suggested, "to rightwise", which doesn't seem a good idea. ("Make righteous" won't quite do because it comes too close to suggesting that the person concerned actually has their moral character transformed, whereas Paul is talking about a change of status rather than a change of character.)

God is doing two closely related things

The second clarification concerns the use of such similar language for God's demonstration of his own righteousness *and* for his justification of sinners. If God is in fact doing two things, why does Paul confuse the situation by using the same vocabulary? The answer is that the justification of sinners through faith in Jesus Christ follows directly from God's own righteousness. God demonstrates his righteousness (he keeps his covenant promises) by declaring those who put their faith in Jesus Christ to be righteous, that is—whether they are Jews or Gentiles—to be members of his covenant family and "in the right" before him. God must act righteously (how could he not?), and in order to act righteously (to be faithful to his promises) he must find a way to bring both Jewish and Gentile believers together in one family apart from the Jewish Law. If he fails to do that, then he has failed to keep his promise to Abraham that he would be the father of many nations (Genesis 17:5) and has failed to act righteously. The righteousness of God and the justification of sinners are different but closely related things.

This is exactly what Paul goes on to point out in the following verses in Romans 3:

> For we hold that one is justified by faith apart from works of the law. Or is God the God of Jews only? Is he not the God of Gentiles also? Yes, of Gentiles also, since God is one—who will justify the circumcised by faith and the uncircumcised through faith.
>
> *Romans 3:28–30*

God is one: he is the God not only of Jews but of Gentiles, which means he wants one covenant family. "Works of the law" cannot, therefore, be the means of justification because that would automatically exclude Gentiles; and anyway, Paul has already pointed out that:

> . . . by works of the law no human being will be justified in his sight, since through the law comes knowledge of sin.
>
> *Romans 3:20*

What he means by "works of the law" we will come to shortly. Why all this matters so much Paul then proceeds to clarify in Romans 4, where he tackles the story of Abraham, showing that Abraham was counted righteous before God by faith before he was circumcised, thus indicating the purpose of God that, in due course, justification should be by faith for all.

The significance of Paul's appeal to Abraham

In much traditional Protestant exegesis Paul's handling of the Abraham story has been treated as no more than a convenient scriptural example of someone being justified by faith. It is as if Paul ran through his mental concordance of Old Testament texts and lighted on Abraham as a good peg to hang his doctrine on: a proof text to demonstrate that justification by faith had some precedent. In fact, it is much more than that. The point about Abraham is that he was chosen to be the beginning of God's rescue plan for creation: the call of Abraham in Genesis 12 to be the means of blessing "all the families of the earth"[18] is God's response to the destructive invasion of sin which is leading humanity into ever more disastrous acts of godlessness and rebellion. The promises to Abraham are the bedrock of the scriptural narrative: take them away, or leave them unfulfilled, and the whole thing collapses into meaninglessness. That is presumably why Jesus is recorded as saying:

> Your father Abraham rejoiced that he would see my day. He saw
> it and was glad.
>
> *John 8:56*

God was keeping his promises and Abraham rejoiced.

Apparent support for the traditional Protestant view

I have said that there are several strands to the case for reading the righteousness of God as his own righteous conduct. We have looked briefly at the argument of Romans as Paul unfolds this theme. We now need to look at the other principal New Testament texts claimed as evidence for the traditional Protestant view of the righteousness of God.

There are four Pauline texts which are usually held to support the doctrine that the righteousness of God or Christ is imputed to those who believe: Romans 4:3–8, 1 Corinthians 1:30, 2 Corinthians 5:21, and Philippians 3:8–9. We will consider each of these.

First, the passage from Romans 4:

> . . . what does the Scripture say? "Abraham believed God, and it was counted to him as righteousness." Now to the one who works, his wages are not counted as a gift but as his due. And to the one who does not work but believes in him who justifies the ungodly, his faith is counted as righteousness, just as David also speaks of the blessing of the one to whom God counts righteousness apart from works:
> "Blessed are those whose lawless deeds are forgiven,
>   and whose sins are covered;
> blessed is the man against whom the
>   Lord will not count his sin."
>
> *Romans 4:3–8*

This is obviously a key text for the meaning of justification. Clearly, it says that God counted Abraham righteous on the basis of his faith; what it does *not* say is that the righteousness *of God or Christ* was imputed to Abraham. That idea is simply not there.

Second, 1 Corinthians 1:30:

> . . . because of him you are in Christ Jesus, who became to us wisdom from God, righteousness and sanctification and redemption.

Paul is listing some of the things which believers have because they are
"in Christ". But that is not the same thing as saying that they have Christ's
own righteousness imputed to them, not least because that would mean
we would have to say that everything else in the list is also imputed to
believers: his wisdom, his sanctification, and his redemption. That doesn't
work because they are different kinds of things: righteousness is a status,
sanctification is a process, and redemption is an event.[19] The passage is
too brief and compact to base a whole doctrine on.

Third, Philippians 3:8–9:

> . . . For [Christ Jesus my Lord's] sake I have suffered the loss of all
> things and count them as rubbish, in order that I may gain Christ
> and be found in him, not having a righteousness of my own that
> comes from the law, but that which comes through faith in Christ,
> the righteousness from God that depends on faith.

The key phrase is "righteousness from God". Not the righteousness *of* God
but righteousness *from* God. All that we can deduce from this text is that
righteousness is God's gift to those who have faith in Christ. Nothing is
said about God's *own* righteousness being imputed to the believer. As
with the passage in Romans 4, the idea is simply not there.

Finally, we come to 2 Corinthians 5:21:[20]

> For our sake he made him to be sin who knew no sin, so that in
> him we might become the righteousness of God.

At first sight, this looks like a clincher for the traditional view of imputed
righteousness: Christ takes our sin and in exchange we receive his
righteousness. Enough said, case closed. If this were correct, then the
doctrine of imputed righteousness would have a solid foundation, and
we would have good reason to read all the other relevant texts in the light
of this one. But things are not that simple: we need to look more closely
at what Paul is saying and the context in which he says it.

Becoming the righteousness of God

Chapters 2–6 of this letter are an extended defence of Paul's ministry as an
apostle. He has been criticized in Corinth as being shabby, unimpressive,
and subject to far too much pain and suffering to be the kind of apostle
they would want to endorse. In reply, Paul explains at length why it is
that his ministry looks the way it does. Essentially what he says is that
proclaiming the cross involves embodying the cross—the dying and rising
of Jesus must be seen in those who preach it; proclamation and life must
match each other because that is how the gospel is communicated and
the Kingdom advanced. Preachers must practise what they preach—not
just in the usual sense of keeping their noses clean but in the much larger
sense of accepting the suffering which comes with the task.

The verse we are looking at is the climax of a series of four two-step
statements in verses 14–21, each of which follows the same pattern:

1. a statement about the death of Jesus
2. a statement about the kind of life and ministry which flow from
    that death.

Because this is such a pivotal issue we will need to look at these verses
in some detail. To make that as easy as possible I have set out the whole
passage with the four two-step statements marked by bracketed numbers,
and the second part of the statement in italics:

> [14] For the love of Christ controls us, because we have concluded
> this: that one has died for all, therefore all have died;
>
> [15] [1] and he died for all, *that those who live might no longer live
> for themselves but for him who for their sake died and was raised.*
>
> [16] From now on, therefore, we regard no one according to
> the flesh. Even though we once regarded Christ according to the
> flesh, we regard him thus no longer.
>
> [17] Therefore, if anyone is in Christ, he is a new creation. The
> old has passed away; behold, the new has come.
>
> [18] [2] All this is from God, who through Christ reconciled us
> to himself *and gave us the ministry of reconciliation;*

[19] that is, [3] in Christ God was reconciling the world to himself, not counting their trespasses against them, *and entrusting to us the message of reconciliation.*

[20] Therefore, we are ambassadors for Christ, God making his appeal through us. We implore you on behalf of Christ, be reconciled to God.

[21] [4] For our sake he made him to be sin who knew no sin, *so that in him we might become the righteousness of God.*

2 Corinthians 5:14–21

Verses 20 and 21 form the conclusion of Paul's argument, signalled by the word "Therefore". Most English versions import a "you" into verse 20 which is not found in any Greek manuscript. As translated in the version quoted here, this looks like an evangelistic appeal. But the Corinthians have already responded to the gospel and don't need to be reconciled to God. Paul is not telling them they need to be converted again; he is describing his apostolic ministry. Verse 20 should rightly be translated along these lines (my translation):

> Therefore, we are ambassadors for Christ, God making his appeal through us. We implore *people* on behalf of Christ: be reconciled to God.

Why does Paul do this? What is the motivation for his apostolic ministry? The fourth and final two-step statement gives the answer:

> For our sake God made him to be sin who knew no sin, *so that in him we might become the righteousness of God.*
>
> *verse 21*

Here we have, at the climax of the series, a striking—even shocking—expression of the meaning of the cross: the total identification of the sinless Messiah with sinful humanity. This is then matched with an equally striking (and exactly parallel) expression of the ministry which flows from the cross: the total identification of the ministers of the gospel with the purpose of God. In the Messiah, God identifies with us in our sin so that we in turn may identify with him in his project of salvation from sin. Paul's apostolic task is nothing less than *the embodiment and enactment of the righteousness of God, that is, his faithfulness to his covenant promises.*

2 Corinthians 5:21 has long been interpreted as describing an exchange: my sin exchanged for God's righteousness. Letting go of that understanding of this verse is likely to be a wrench for some readers. It seems such a powerful expression of what Jesus has done for us. But the interpretation I have been outlining doesn't in any way detract from the reality of that exchange. God really does take away my sin through the cross and grants me a righteous status instead. What the fresh interpretation does is to take that window on the cross and open it wide to an altogether larger perspective. There is indeed an exchange which Paul is talking about, but at this moment it is not my sin for God's righteousness; rather, it is my sin for a share in the saving purpose of God. Not only has God dealt with my sinfulness; above and beyond that, he is involving me in his mission. I have not only been rescued from the scrapheap; I have been included in the team that goes on rescuing other people from the same scrapheap. That is arguably an even better deal than the one put before us by the traditional exegesis.

I hope this survey of some relevant New Testament texts is enough to point out some of the difficulties of the traditional Protestant understanding of the righteousness of God, and to indicate that the fresh interpretation currently being espoused by some scholars has a lot going for it.

The faithfulness of God to his covenant promises

If, then, the righteousness of God is his own righteous conduct and refers particularly to his faithfulness to his covenant promises, how is this worked out in the events concerning Jesus of Nazareth?

God had promised Abraham that he would make him into a great nation, and "in you all the families of the earth shall be blessed." Abraham and his descendants were designed to be God's answer to the rising tide of sin described in Genesis 3–11.

But in Romans 2 Paul shows how Israel is just as guilty of sin as the nations are. Instead of being the solution to the human predicament, they are part of the problem. And they have failed in their vocation to be the vehicle of God's revelation to the world. They were "entrusted with the oracles of God"[21] but they treated this vocation as something to boast about instead of a sacred trust to be followed through with diligence and humility: they not only missed the mark of living in obedience to God's law; they missed the point of their calling.

The faithful Israelite

Has God's promise to Abraham failed? Is that the end of his covenant with Israel? Not at all, says Paul. The faithlessness of Israel was no surprise to God and did not force him either to abandon his purpose or to resort to Plan B. His purpose will still go forward to its glorious conclusion and still through Israel, but *through Israel embodied in one person*—the one faithful Israelite:

> But now the righteousness of God has been manifested apart from the Law, although the Law and the Prophets bear witness to it— the righteousness of God through the faithfulness of Jesus Christ for all who believe.
>
> **Romans 3:21–22 (my translation)**

Traditionally, the words rendered here as "through the faithfulness of Jesus Christ" have been translated "through faith in Jesus Christ". However, the Greek word *pistis* can mean either "faith" or "faithfulness" according to context, and the "faithfulness of Jesus Christ" is a more literal translation than "faith in Jesus Christ". Crucially, in this context, "the faithfulness of Jesus Christ" answers exactly to Israel's failure to produce the needed faithfulness.[22]

Later in the letter, in Romans 5, Paul writes of the *obedience* of Jesus, by which he undoes the disobedience of Adam:

> . . . as by one man's disobedience the many were made sinners,
> so by the one man's obedience the many will be made righteous.
>
> **Romans 5:19**

Obedience and faithfulness are two facets of the same reality: two ways of looking at our response to God. Israel failed in its vocation of obedient faithfulness. The faithful obedience of the one faithful Israelite filled the gap. This is so crucial to the theology of the whole New Testament—not just Paul but Jesus and the Gospel writers too—that it is important to understand that this was always the way it was going to be. It was not a desperate remedy for a plot that had gone wrong: it was the very heart of the plot. The theme of Israel's vocation devolving on to one person is deeply embedded in Israel's scriptures.

The vocation of Israel focused in one person

In Daniel Chapter 7, Daniel has a dream. Like Nebuchadnezzar's dream in Chapter 2, the dream gives a symbolic portrayal of four successive kingdoms, the last of which is succeeded by the arrival of the Kingdom of God to destroy all other claims to kingship. In Daniel's dream the four kingdoms are represented by four vicious beasts. The climax of the dream is "one like a Son of Man" being presented to God to be given the kingdom which will never be destroyed (a key passage we looked at in Chapter 1):

> I saw in the night visions,
> and behold, with the clouds of heaven
>   there came one like a son of man,
> and he came to the Ancient of Days
>   and was presented before him.

And to him was given dominion
    and glory and a kingdom,
that all peoples, nations, and languages
    should serve him;
his dominion is an everlasting dominion,
    which shall not pass away,
and his kingdom one
    that shall not be destroyed.

Daniel 7:13–14

Daniel is disturbed by his dream and approaches a bystander (presumably an angel) for the interpretation. The answer he gets is this:

These four great beasts are four kings who shall rise out of the earth. But *the saints of the Most High* shall receive the kingdom and possess the kingdom forever, forever and ever.

Daniel 7:17–18 (my italics)

The angel identifies "one like a Son of Man" with "the saints of the Most High". They are one and the same: the Son of Man represents or embodies the saints of the Most High.

Israel in person

"Son of Man" was Jesus' favoured self-designation. He uses it more than any other self-description—by a very large margin. On a few occasions he refers to himself as "the Son" (particularly, but not exclusively, in John's Gospel), implying that he has a unique relationship with God. But he refers to himself as "the Son of Man" twenty-nine times in Matthew's Gospel alone. It looks as if, whatever else Jesus intended, he certainly had the figure of Daniel 7 in mind. He believed himself to be the representative of God's people. As Tom Wright puts it, he believed himself to be "Israel-in-person". He is the one in whom Israel's destiny is summed up and worked out, the one who takes upon himself the vocation which Israel was both unwilling and unable to fulfil.

One stands in for the many

This theme of one person representing or standing in for a whole nation may seem to those of us in the individualistic culture of the West contrived and unreal. But a moment's thought will show that, in fact, this is an idea we are well used to and which moves us profoundly. Countless fictional narratives—novels, films, TV series—hinge on an apparently hopeless situation where one character comes alone to the rescue: saving a loved one, a family, a community, a nation, even the world, against all the odds, through their own courage and resourcefulness. It is one of the most enduringly popular of all plots. It's a storyline which touches us so deeply because it is archetypal; it is an intimation of the greatest story of all—the triumph of one man, crucified in weakness but rising in glory, not over some local or temporary disaster, but over all that threatens the well-being of the world, including death itself.

The justification of sinners

So much for the question of the real meaning of the righteousness of God and its outworking through the faithfulness of Jesus the Messiah. We need now to explore the other kind of righteousness—the justification of sinners—which was the second of the two achievements of the cross, according to Romans 3:25–26:

> ... This was to show God's righteousness, because in his divine
> forbearance he had passed over former sins. It was to show his

> righteousness at the present time, so that he might be just and
> the justifier of the one who has faith in Jesus.

I have attempted to make the case that the "imputed righteousness" view of justification doesn't really work. If that is the case, what *is* justification about and how *does* it work?

It is generally agreed that justification is God bringing forward *into the present* the verdict pronounced at the *future final* judgement of all humans.[23] He is bringing the assurance of final vindication before the judgement throne of God into the present experience of the believer. It is the divine declaration that this person is now, in the present time, "righteous"—not that their character is righteous, good, or virtuous but that they have a right standing before God, having been acquitted of guilt in the divine law court. They are "in the right". It's a bit like the fortunate young person who is offered an unconditional place at their preferred university before they take their A levels. The verdict is known in advance of their actual exam results. The place is theirs even if their grades are less than brilliant.

Justified in Christ

All this follows from our faith-relationship with Jesus. We are justified *in Christ*.[24] That is why Paul speaks of his desire to be "found in him".[25] We are vindicated by God because he was vindicated by God, and we are in him. What is true of him is true of those who are in him.

This, I suspect, is the truth which the Christmas Day illustration I quoted earlier is trying to communicate. In that scenario, Jesus gives his righteousness to the unrighteous sinner faced with a holy God. The idea is that "the righteousness of Christ" is given in exchange for the believer's sin. But the New Testament never, in fact, speaks of "the righteousness *of* Christ", despite popular misconceptions to the contrary. It says instead that we are "justified/righteous *in* Christ."[26] Having been united with Christ by faith and baptism, we enjoy the status that he enjoys. It is not that he has built up a store of righteousness through living a perfect life on earth which he can dispense to those in need. It is simply that he is the Father's beloved Son and nothing can disrupt or diminish the perfection of their relationship, and we are incorporated into that relationship. More than that, God has vindicated Jesus by raising him from the dead and, being in Christ, we share in his vindication.

You can, if you want, choose to speak of the righteousness of Christ being imputed to the believer. But the language of justification in Christ is more scriptural and encourages us to explore and enjoy the full richness of what it means to be incorporated into the Messiah.

Corporate solidarity and Western individualism

The reason for the Western church's neglect of language about being "in Christ" may be that the kind of corporate solidarity involved is foreign to our individualistic culture. Or we think it is. In fact, I think corporate solidarity is something we understand very well. This is what we are experiencing when our team wins a match and we say, "We won!" even though most of us were not on the pitch or even necessarily present in the ground when the match took place. We identify with the team: what is true of them (whether they won or lost, did well or performed disastrously) is true of us too.

Corporate solidarity is a reality of the human condition. We are not merely isolated individuals: we belong to, identify with, are implicated in and share the fate of a whole range of human communities at many different levels and in many different ways.

Justification in practice

I want to suggest that Paul's letters give us one example of how justification works out in practice—in Paul's account of the faith of Abraham in Romans 4. I do this with some hesitation because the commentators don't (as far as I have been able to discover) notice this. But here goes anyway.

This is the passage in question:

> He [Abraham] did not weaken in faith when he considered his own body, which was as good as dead (since he was about a hundred years old), or when he considered the barrenness of Sarah's womb. No distrust made him waver concerning the promise of God, but he grew strong in his faith as he gave glory to God, fully convinced that God was able to do what he had promised.
>
> *Romans 4:19–21*

This strikes me as a rather optimistic account of Abraham's faith. Yes, he believed the promise of God, but did he never weaken in faith? Is it accurate to claim that "no distrust made him waver", that "he was fully convinced" that God would deliver on his promises? The relevant chapters of Genesis tell a more down-to-earth story of someone who did quite often waver in faith, a story much more like the story of most of us who claim to have faith in God. I think Paul is presenting us with the edited version of Abraham's life. The sins, the wrong turnings, the failures of faith have been airbrushed out. I suggest that, because of the cross, God will do the same for all of us who put our trust in his Son. Our sins, the ways we have fallen short of what God intended for us, are covered by the sacrifice of Christ.

Justification by faith in Galatians

We have seen that the righteousness of God in Paul's language is about the faithfulness of God to his covenant promises. It is about covenant and how covenant works out in practice. When Paul uses the language of justification/righteousness in reference to humans, he is also talking about the covenant promises of God.

All this is worked out in detail by Paul in his letter to the Galatians, which is where the first New Testament discussion of justification is found. Paul begins his discussion with a concrete example of how justification works in practice: the story of his confrontation with Peter.

The scene is Antioch. The new church consists of both Jews and Gentiles, both of whom have come to believe in Jesus as Messiah. As a result they are eating together—that is, they have set aside the taboo which decrees that Jews have no dealings with Gentiles.[27] They have effectively abolished the boundary marker which separated Israel from the rest of the world, marking out the Jews alone as God's people. Observing the food laws had been one of the ways you knew who was in the covenant and who was not. That doesn't work any more because Jews and Gentiles who believe in the Messiah are eating at the same table.

When Peter arrives on the scene, he happily joins in.[28] He had learned from the vision recounted in Acts 10 and his experience in the house of Cornelius that the old food laws were no longer relevant. The voice from heaven had told him clearly:

"What God has made clean, do not call common."

Acts 10:15

But then a delegation arrives in Antioch from Jerusalem and Peter loses his nerve. Fearful of what the Jerusalem believers will think of his sharing a table with Gentiles, he draws back and separates himself from them.

Paul will have none of it. He confronts Peter:

"If you, though a Jew, live like a Gentile and not like a Jew, how can you force the Gentiles to live like Jews?"

Galatians 2:14

Paul is pointing out the implication of Peter's action in separating himself from the Gentile believers. By happily eating with Gentiles, Peter had been tacitly acknowledging that these Gentile fellow-believers were on an equal footing within the covenant with himself as a Jew by birth. By then refusing to eat with Gentile believers, he was implying that they would have to become Jews to be full members of the covenant.

Paul proceeds to explain how radically unacceptable Peter's action is:

> We ourselves are Jews by birth and not Gentile sinners; yet we know that a person is not justified by works of the Law but through the faithfulness of Jesus Christ, so we also have believed in Christ Jesus, in order to be justified through the faithfulness of Christ and not by works of the Law, because by works of the Law no one will be justified.
>
> ### Galatians 2:15–16 (my translation)

By withdrawing from table fellowship with Gentile believers, Peter was reverting to the old basis for being declared righteous: the works of the Law. That, says Paul, is no good: nobody is going to be declared righteous on that basis.

The meaning of "works of the Law"

What does Paul mean by "works of the Law"? The standard Protestant Reformation interpretation is that this refers to the human attempt to gain acceptance with God by keeping the moral law: being as good as you can in the hope of chalking up enough moral merit to get you into heaven.

There are (at least) two problems with this.

Firstly, it is unlikely that Paul ever believed you could earn merit with God like that. The Law was never intended to be a ladder for God's people to climb to achieve acceptance with him. The Law was given to those already at the top of the ladder, those who had *already* been redeemed from slavery in Egypt, who were *already* secure in their status as his people, as the Ten Commandments make very clear:

> And God spoke all these words, saying,
>> "I am the Lord your God, who brought you out of the land of Egypt, out of the house of slavery."
>
> *Exodus 20:1–2*

Therefore, this is the way you should live:

> You shall have no other gods before me *[etc.]*.
>
> *Exodus 20:3ff*

The Law was not *a road to salvation* but *a road to be followed by those who were already being saved.*

Secondly, the context in Galatians makes it clear that "works of the Law" means something much more specific and restricted than a generalized concern for keeping the moral law to justify yourself. In Galatians, "works of the Law" are "living like a Jew"[29] and avoiding having dealings—including sharing a table—with "Gentile sinners".[30] What Peter had learned from his vision in Acts 10 was not that the moral law was now irrelevant, or had ceased to be the means of salvation (which it never was), but that those aspects of the Jewish Law which separated Jew from Gentile were now irrelevant and to be ditched accordingly. Jesus himself "declared all foods clean" (Mark 7:19), not because the Law had made a mistake in banning certain foods, but because the Law had done its job and a new age was dawning, in which Jew and Gentile would come together in one body.

Uniting Jew and Gentile in one single family of God

In Galatians 3 Paul goes to great lengths to expound Genesis 17:19, to the effect that the covenant promises were made "to Abraham and his [single] seed".

One of the meanings of the Greek word for "seed" is "family", and Paul's concern is that nothing should get in the way of God's plan to fulfil his promise to Abraham to create a single, world-wide family. If justification is by works of the Law, then that cannot happen—the Law will create two families: one Jewish and one Gentile. If that were to happen, not only would the promise to Abraham fail, but the divine purpose to restore the unity of the human race (fractured by sin) would fail too. That would be "a different gospel",[31] which Paul will resist at all costs.

The Reformation rightly protested against the mistaken late medieval belief that you could earn God's acceptance by means of your moral achievement. But all the evidence suggests that this is not what Paul was confronting Peter about, or what his doctrine of justification sought to challenge.

When Paul expounds justification he has two primary concerns: to safeguard the purpose of God to create a single family which brings Jew and Gentile together on an equal footing, and to show how God deals with the problem of sin, since the Law can never justify anybody because it exposes sin rather than defeating it. The situation he is addressing at the time will determine which of those two concerns dominates in any given context.

Some reflections

What difference does all this make? Here are seven suggestions.

1. The vindication of God

So far in this book we have explored Jesus' proclamation of the Kingdom of God and Paul's theme of the righteousness of God. Both themes are about the vindication of God—his own vindication of himself. The Kingdom theme is the vindication of his *government of the cosmos*: despite any appearance to the contrary, he is in charge of his creation and is moving his purposes forward to fulfilment. The righteousness theme is the vindication of his *faithfulness to his promises*. The Kingdom theme emphasizes the action of God in working to restore his world; the righteousness theme emphasizes the action of God in fulfilling his covenant with Israel. The two themes come together and complement each other in several ways. Centrally, they come together in the person of Jesus Christ, the Son of Man who fulfils *both* the Danielic prophecies of the coming of the Kingdom *and* the promise to Abraham that in him all the families of the earth would be blessed. Both themes tell a story, again centred on the person of Jesus Christ who comes "to destroy the works of the devil",[32] a story of liberation from sin and consequent cosmic renewal.

Disentangling Paul's theme of the righteousness of God from the traditional Protestant view (that it's about his righteousness being credited to believers) enables us to see clearly the parallelism between the story Jesus tells and the story Paul tells. They are essentially the same story but seen from different standpoints. Covenant and Kingdom are two sides of the same coin, two ways of looking at the purpose and action of God towards his creation.

2. The gospel of God

The gospel, Paul tells us, reveals the righteousness of God. In that case, the gospel is before all else about God and his concerns, and not about me and mine. The old Protestant view of the righteousness of God being primarily about God transferring his righteousness to the sinner obscured this truth. It pictured God and his gospel revolving around my need for forgiveness (which is real and important), whereas Paul wants to tell us that the gospel is God acting in faithfulness to himself—his covenant promises. The gospel is a summons from God to repentance and faith, not a consumer-oriented special offer which we are invited to consider. It is a call to obedience rather than an option we might want to buy into. It is the King calling his rebellious subjects to order.

Evangelists and preachers need confidence that they are announcing important news rather than competing for attention in the media marketplace. If our whole strategy for bringing people to faith is based on engaging people's sense of need, we are selling the gospel short: those who don't have a sense of need can quite easily dismiss our message. Not, of course, that our preaching should be harsh or careless of people's felt needs; we just need to know that we are communicating a divine command.

3. The faithfulness of Jesus

We have seen that some key passages in Paul which have been traditionally understood as referring to *faith in* Jesus are better read as speaking of the *faithfulness of* Jesus. One of the good things about that is that it shifts the focus from us to him. What we are relying on is not our faith but his faithfulness. We do not place our trust in our faith but in him and his faithfulness. This, I suggest, takes the pressure off. We can put down the burden of trying to rustle up enough faith and let him take the strain. If faith becomes self-focused ("How much faith have I got? How real is my faith?"), it is in danger of ceasing to be real faith at all. Faith finds its proper object outside of myself and in Jesus. There will be more to say about this when we come in a later chapter to think further about the importance of faith in the life of discipleship.

4. The nature of the church

In exploring justification we have seen that this is as much about the nature of the church as it is about our standing with God: in fact, those two things are two ways of looking at the *same* thing. To be in good standing with God is to be a member of his covenant family, the church.

And the boundary marker, the sign that tells us who is a member of this covenant family, is faith in Jesus Christ. Everything else is irrelevant: gender, social class, ethnicity, socio-economic status, etc. This is one of the ways the church is so special. It unites human beings as nothing else does. The church is not a club for the like-minded, a group for those who share the same interests, or a gathering of "people like us". When it becomes any of these, something has gone wrong. When the church is not uniting people who would never otherwise associate with each other, it is failing to fulfil the purpose for which it was created. The church is a family brought together by shared allegiance to Jesus Christ. The actual composition of any local congregation is important. Which sections of the community are not represented, or under-represented, and why? The church needs to ask itself: are we setting up, even unconsciously, boundaries which exclude certain kinds of people? The only boundary marker which God recognizes is faith in Jesus Christ. Wherever people manifest this faith, we have a duty to welcome and love them as brothers and sisters. Of course, that is far from simple. But we too easily lose sight of how central this is to being the church.

5. Communicating the gospel

How is the gospel supposed to be communicated? Christians tend to divide into those who emphasize proclamation (what we say) and those who emphasize action (what we do). What we have seen in looking closely at Paul's account of his own ministry in 2 Corinthians 5 is that you can't separate the two. He both speaks the gospel and embodies the gospel. He speaks good news, but as well as that he *is* good news. That is one implication of Paul's daring words about "becoming the righteousness of God". Every church must not only proclaim the good news of Jesus but must ensure that they *are* good news to their locality. I remember a church leader recounting how he prayed about which among a range of possible practical projects his church should adopt as a means of blessing their community; he felt God say to him, "Just do *something*."

6. Understanding the Old Testament

The Old Testament is widely neglected today in churches and among Christians. People don't know it, and often they don't like the little they know. Getting a grasp of covenant is one of the principal remedies for this disease, because covenant holds together the two Testaments as one single story rather than merely a collection of stories.

This is a deeply and unalterably Jewish story. One of the greatest sins of Christendom and the Christian church is the recurrent appearance of anti-Semitism. Theologians have not always helped in this: too often they have sought to distance both Jesus and Paul from their Jewish roots. I hope this chapter has shown that you can't do that. Perhaps if that were more widely understood the horror of "Christian" anti-Semitism could be avoided.

7. Appreciating St Paul

Finally, covenant helps us to appreciate Paul as a thinker and writer of enormous stature. Until we understand his appeal to the story of Abraham, in Romans and Galatians, as part of a coherent theology of covenant, much of what he writes looks like an unprincipled use of bits of Old Testament scripture chosen almost at random. Sometimes, as in his intricate discussion of Abraham's "seed" in Galatians 3, he appears to be playing games with words which we find hard to engage with. This does nothing for the respect we give him or the diligence with which we read his letters. By painstakingly uncovering the underlying structure and flow of Paul's thought, Tom Wright's covenant-based approach demonstrates how rich and compelling those letters really are.

CHAPTER 3

Cross

In the previous chapter we explored Paul's use of covenant as his basic framework for understanding the purpose of God in the gospel. We saw that Paul's use of covenant hinges on his discovery that, in the person of Jesus of Nazareth, a faithful Israelite has arisen to fulfil the purpose which Israel itself failed to fulfil. And this was not Plan B, a response to a new situation hastily put together by a God caught out by the unexpected failure of Israel; rather, this was the way it was always going to be. God had it in mind from the beginning to save the world through Israel's anointed King, the Messiah, his own incarnate Son.

Paul is interpreting the story of Jesus within the larger story of Israel. He is saying that the events concerning Jesus of Nazareth can only be rightly understood as part of the long-range plan of God for putting the world right which began with the call of Abraham. The story of Jesus means what it means as the continuation and fulfilment of the story of Israel, and *only* as the continuation and fulfilment of that story. Insert the story of Jesus into any other story or try to interpret it within any other framework or theory, and it will not make the sense it was intended to make.

The cross and the story of Israel

The same principle holds good for the meaning of the cross.[33] The cross means what it means within the story of Israel. That's what Paul has in mind when he tells the Corinthians:

> For I delivered to you as of first importance what I also received:
> that Christ died for our sins *in accordance with the Scriptures.*
>
> *1 Corinthians 15:3 (my italics)*

Paul makes it clear that this is not just his idea. It is the shared understanding of the earliest followers of Jesus and as such was a key element in the tradition which Paul received and passed on to the churches.

According to Luke's Gospel, this way of interpreting the cross goes back to Jesus himself—in his conversations with the two disciples on the road to Emmaus and with the eleven back in Jerusalem:

> And he said to them, "O foolish ones, and slow of heart to believe
> all that the prophets have spoken! Was it not necessary that the
> Christ should suffer these things and enter into his glory?" And
> beginning with Moses and all the Prophets, he interpreted to
> them in all the Scriptures the things concerning himself.
>
> *Luke 24:25–27*

Luke doesn't tell us how Jesus interpreted the scriptures as referring to himself. But if we attend carefully both to the story of Israel and to the story told by the Gospels and Paul, we can trace something of how the one is reflected and fulfilled in the other.

I suggest that the story of Israel can be summed up in three words:

1. Election
2. Exodus
3. Exile

We can further sum up the meaning of the story of Israel in three more words:

1. Election is about *focus*.
2. Exodus is about *freedom*.
3. Exile is about *forgiveness*.

First, Election—in the sense of its root meaning of "choice" from which, of course, the familiar usage in relation to political and other elections derives.

The story of Israel: Election

The history of Israel begins with God's Election of Abraham to be the means of blessing "all the families of the earth". Sin has invaded and spoilt God's creation. God's answer to the problem is to *focus* his response on one man, and the family which that one man will bring into being. Abraham's family is to be the means of restoring creation to its original purpose.

The story not only begins with Election: Election is also the means by which it develops. Abraham has two sons: Ishmael and Isaac. But the focus of God is on Isaac alone. Similarly, Isaac has two sons: Esau and Jacob. But the focus of God is on Jacob alone. It is Jacob's family which is to be the means of achieving the saving purpose of God.

Fast forward to the period of the monarchy and the process of Election continues: during the reign of Solomon's successor Rehoboam, Israel is torn apart, divided between ten tribes in the North and two in the South. The northern tribes turn away from the Lord and so Election focuses on the southern kingdom alone. The southern kingdom also soon turns away from the Lord, and the people are sent into exile in Babylon. And so the process of Election further narrows the focus to the remnant who return to the Land after seventy years in exile.

During the period of exile and the subsequent return to the Land, prophetic voices in the books of Daniel and Isaiah begin to speak of a yet more drastic phase in the process of Election, where the purpose of God narrows down to focus on a single individual. As we saw in Chapter 2, Daniel sees "one like a Son of Man" representing and embodying the entire people of Israel. And in Isaiah 40–55 we find the figure of the Servant, who in some passages is Israel as a nation, and in others is a single individual.

The climax of this long process of Election comes in Isaiah 53, when the Servant—now utterly alone—bears the sins of the many: "the LORD has laid on him the iniquity of us all."[34] The sinful story of Israel finally comes crashing down on one person.

This is the story which Paul picks up when he develops the theme of the Messiah's faithfulness filling the gap left by Israel's unfaithfulness. The long story of Election progressively narrows the focus of God's purposes to the single person of his Son. This was not a last-minute decision but the way the story developed all along.

Thoughtful people sometimes ask how it is that the death of one individual a long time ago can have anything to do with us. How can one man's sacrifice save the whole world from sin? What is the connection between the death of Jesus around AD 30 and my sin two thousand years later? The theme of Election helps us to understand. Just as Election shows us how the *story of Israel* devolves on to one person, so it also shows how the *sin of the world* lands on one person. It shows—to use Tom Wright's phrase—how sin is "heaped up in one place".[35]

Sin focused in one place

This is how it works. Abraham and his descendants are chosen to represent the human race in undoing the sin of Adam. By the long process I have described, Abraham's descendants are narrowed down to the person of Jesus. And humanity decides to put him to death—loading on to the sinless Son of God its own rejection of God.

The crucifixion of Jesus of Nazareth is the ultimate sinful act. To put to death the sinless Son of God, the one who has done nothing except offer freedom, forgiveness, healing, and blessing, the one who has spoken only grace and truth: this is sin at its most sinful, sin in its most concentrated form, distilled to its very essence. The essence of sin, says Jesus, is this:

> " . . . they do not believe in me."
>
> *John 16:9*

Not believing in him they reject and crucify him.

Sin at its most sinful is not simply wrongdoing, but wrongdoing that is *known* to be wrongdoing. It is the breaking of a commandment: transgressing—that is, stepping over—a clearly marked line in the sand. This was part of the mysterious but gracious purpose of God in giving the Law to Israel:

> . . . the law came in to increase the trespass.
>
> *Romans 5:20*

> So the law is holy, and the commandment is holy and righteous and good.
>
> Did that which is good, then, bring death to me? By no means! It was sin, producing death in me through what is good, in order that *sin might be shown to be sin*, and through the commandment might *become sinful beyond measure*.
>
> *Romans 7:12–13 (my italics)*

The Law was given with the specific purpose of revealing and gathering into one place the full sinfulness of sin. The Law "increases the trespass", makes it absolutely plain that sin is indeed sin, makes sin "sinful beyond measure", thus making it possible to deal with sin fully and finally. The primal sin of Adam was the transgression of an explicit divine commandment. The sin of Israel in sending her Messiah to a Roman cross is likewise the transgression of her God-given Law. Israel recapitulates the primal sin of humanity (and is aided and abetted in that by the pagan power of Rome). That is both her tragedy and her glory: the tragedy of involvement in sin at its most sinful and the glory of being the means by which God works salvation from sin.

The most striking expression of this focusing of sin in one place is Paul's statement in 2 Corinthians 5:21:

> For our sake he [God] made him to be sin who knew no sin . . .

Jesus of Nazareth takes upon himself the sin of the whole world. The sinless one is wholly identified with sin: sin is wholly concentrated in him and upon him. Sin is gathered up and cornered, which means it can be decisively dealt with—once and for all.

Having gathered sin into one place, God condemned it—passed judicial sentence on it—in the flesh of his Son. Sin was judged and punished:

> For God has done what the law, weakened by the flesh, could not
> do. By sending his own Son in the likeness of sinful flesh and for
> sin, he condemned sin in the flesh.
>
> ***Romans 8:3***

At this point it is worth answering another question which thoughtful people often raise. How can God be responsible for sending his Son to the cross? How can a just God unload the sin of the world on to his sinless Son? Is that not the most terrible *injustice*?

Here it is important to hold together the witness of the Gospels with the witness of the rest of the New Testament. The Gospels make it abundantly clear that it was humans who loaded their sin on to Jesus, inflicting the most concentrated malice on him and committing the most terrible injustice against him. The sin-bearing of Jesus is not an abstract transaction in the mind of God or in a theological system: it is a datable event. In actual historical fact, humans conspired to lay their sins on the innocent shoulders of Jesus of Nazareth. The wonder is that this was turned round by the grace of God, against all human possibility and contrary to anything anybody could have anticipated, and made the means of salvation. As Joseph tells the brothers who sold him into slavery and reported him dead to their father:

" . . . you meant evil against me, but God meant it for good . . . "

Genesis 50:20

Human evil and divine goodness meet at the cross and divine goodness wins.

Election is about focus; next comes Exodus which, as we will see, is about freedom.

The story of Israel: Exodus

Exodus is the liberation of Abraham's family from slavery in Egypt in order that they may be free to worship God. Under the leadership of Moses the family becomes a nation, leaving the place of bondage to meet with God in the desert of Sinai. There they receive the Law, the national covenant is inaugurated, the tabernacle is constructed and, guided by the pillar of cloud by day and the pillar of fire by night, they begin their journey to the Promised Land. In due course they enter the Land and, once they have defeated the Canaanite inhabitants, the stage is set for the development of their life as a nation and the establishment of the monarchy. It looks as if the nation is all set up to enjoy the freedom which was always God's intention for his people.

But Israel in the time of Jesus is not living in freedom but under oppression. They are ruled by the pagan Roman Empire and their own leaders collaborate with the ruling power. To make matters worse, daily life for a large proportion of the population is dominated by the contempt expressed for them by their religious superiors. But every year the nation remembers that it is supposed to be free. In celebrating the Feast of the Passover the nation is remembering the Exodus and hoping for the day when freedom will come again. Passover was therefore a time of heightened tension for the authorities: Pilate left his normal residence in Caesarea to be in the city in case of trouble, and the Jewish leaders were acutely aware that they could provoke a riot if they arrested Jesus at the wrong time.

In choosing Passover for his showdown with the powers in Jerusalem, Jesus is invoking Exodus as the narrative by which to understand what he is doing. He could have chosen a different occasion, such as the Day of Atonement. He could still have attended the Passover celebration but kept under the radar. Instead he chooses deliberate confrontation by arranging a public and provocative entry into the city which stirred up the enthusiasm of the crowds with its clearly Messianic message of the fulfilment of Zechariah 9:9:

> Rejoice greatly, O daughter of Zion!
>> Shout aloud, O daughter of Jerusalem!
> Behold, your king is coming to you;
>> righteous and having salvation is he,
> humble and mounted on a donkey,
>> on a colt, the foal of a donkey.

Luke tells us that, at the Transfiguration, Moses and Elijah spoke with Jesus "about his exodus, which he was to fulfil at Jerusalem".[36] That is a rather literal translation but it highlights the two key words: "exodus" and "fulfil". The events of the Passion are the deliberate fulfilment of the Exodus story.

Luke also gives us a sense of the importance to Jesus of the Passover setting of his suffering and death. When Jesus sits down to eat the meal with his disciples he tells them:

> "I have earnestly desired to eat this Passover with you before I suffer."
>
> *Luke 22:15*

His words could be literally rendered, "with desire I have desired . . . " Eating *this* Passover with his disciples was no mere performance of a religious duty; it was the focus and fulfilment of a passionate longing to enable the coming of the Kingdom and the liberation of humanity.

Jesus confronts the powers

In fulfilling the Exodus story, Jesus is doing what Moses did at the original Exodus: confronting the powers that enslave—human and non-human. There are the obvious human agents of oppression: Pharaoh in the original Exodus story, Caiaphas and Pilate in the new Exodus. But behind these human agents there are the dark powers which inhabit the heavenly realms and work through (mostly unwitting) human agents.

Jesus' intention to confront the powers in a final showdown should come as no surprise. It fits perfectly within his ministry. As Moses confronts the abusive power of Pharaoh in the events leading up to the Exodus, so Jesus confronts the abusive power of the Jewish authorities. As Moses challenges the dark powers of Pharaoh's magicians, so also Jesus challenges and defeats the demonic powers afflicting the people. In life and in death Jesus does battle with the forces which enslave humanity. The victory of the Kingdom of God is enacted alike in his ministry and his crucifixion.

Careful consideration of the Passion narratives in the Gospels reveals something of the way the human and non-human powers interact. The human powers think they are in control; they think that by putting Jesus to death they have solved their problem and got rid of him. They imagine that Jesus is subject to them and that their purpose will prevail. But there is a sense throughout the Passion narratives that the truth is the other way round. The strong impression is conveyed that Caiaphas, Pilate, and the other actors in the drama are not truly free, not really as much in control of events as they suppose. Pilate, for example, is warned by his wife not to have anything to do with Jesus because he is innocent; he appears to believe her, claiming that by washing his hands he is somehow "innocent of this man's blood";[37] but then he proceeds to have Jesus scourged and to hand him over to be crucified. He fears a riot but doesn't summon the courage to mobilize his troops to deal with a riot (which he did on other occasions). For all his apparent power, Pilate is a man in the grip of circumstances which he can't or won't control.

Similarly, Caiaphas only manages to get Jesus arrested because Jesus allows the arrest to go ahead, and he is then powerless to secure the evidence to present Jesus to the Governor for execution; until, that is,

Jesus himself hands him what he needs with this ringing declaration of confidence in his own coming vindication:

> "I tell you, from now on you will see the Son of Man seated at
> the right hand of Power and coming on the clouds of heaven."
>
> *Matthew 26:64*

Despite appearances, neither Caiaphas nor Pilate is free—they're in the grip of the powers. Despite wielding power in theory, they are in reality the tools of the shadowy spiritual forces which are working out their own purposes through them. Like the Conservative government of John Major in the early 1990s, they are "in office but not in power". They exemplify in practice what the apostle had in mind when he said:

> . . . the whole world lies in the power of the evil one.
>
> *1 John 5:19*

In contrast to Pilate and Caiaphas, Jesus exhibits a mysterious freedom: he often seems to be in charge of unfolding events. After the agony of his prayer in Gethsemane, his peace and clarity of purpose are restored and he walks through the terrible events of the Passion with an extraordinary calm and poise. He speaks few words, sometimes choosing silence instead, but the words he does speak are measured and pointed, full of grace and truth rather than fear or anger. He tells Judas to do what he has come to do; he tells Peter to put his sword away and heals the ear of the high priest's servant, which Peter has cut off; he assures Peter that he could call on legions of angels to defend himself if he chose; he rebukes the arresting party for coming after him with swords and clubs; he rests in the confidence that events will take their course so that the scriptures will be fulfilled.

These are not the actions of one who is a victim of circumstances. He is confronting the powers, not merely the human agents but the hidden forces of darkness which operate through them. He confronts power not with power, but from a position of weakness and vulnerability which, in fact, turns out to be the one position of real strength.

In this, Jesus is again fulfilling the pattern of scripture, notably the story of David and Goliath. David, the anointed but not-yet-enthroned King of Israel, fights the battle on Israel's behalf, standing in for Israel when Israel is too frightened to get the job done, and—alone and defenceless except for his five smooth stones and slingshot—takes on the mighty Philistine. In both cases, "Israel-in-person" confronts the forces of evil from a position of radical vulnerability and emerges victorious. Jesus does what David had done before, only this time the victory is achieved through the Spirit-enabled power of suffering love alone, and is complete and final rather than local and temporary.

Victory over the powers according to Paul

This victory over the enslaving powers of darkness is a central element not only in the Gospels, but also in Paul's understanding of the cross. He tells the Colossians:

> [God] disarmed the rulers and authorities and put them to open
> shame, by triumphing over them in him.
>
> *Colossians 2:15*

Similarly, using the Exodus language of "redemption", he calls the Galatians not to abandon the freedom from enslaving powers won by the Messiah and implemented in the Holy Spirit:

> In the same way we also, when we were children, were enslaved
> to the elementary principles of the world. But when the fullness
> of time had come, God sent forth his Son, born of woman, born
> under the law, to *redeem* those who were under the law . . .
> Formerly, when you did not know God, you were enslaved to
> those that by nature are not gods. But now that you have come
> to know God, or rather to be known by God, how can you turn

back again to the weak and worthless elementary principles of
the world, whose slaves you want to be once more?

Galatians 4:3–5, 8–9 (my italics)

The cross restores to humans the freedom to be what they were designed
to be in the first place.

Free to worship

The point of the Exodus was that Israel should be free to worship God:
at least eight times God says to Pharaoh, "Let my people go, that they
may worship me." The purpose of God is to set people free from the dark
oppressive powers which undermine true worship.

The fundamental issue for humanity is worship. We have often
assumed that the fundamental human problem is sin. In one sense
that is, of course, true. But it needs to be clear that sin stems from false
worship: idolatry. When Paul expounds the wrath of God in Romans 1 his
primary focus is on idolatry: "ungodliness" comes first in his catalogue
of accusations,[38] and the verses immediately following are an extended
exposition of humanity's failure to acknowledge, honour, and thank God
as they should. The climax of the case against humans is this, expressed
with the special emphasis of a doxology and an "Amen":

> . . . they exchanged the truth about God for a lie and worshipped
> and served the creature rather than the Creator, who is blessed
> forever! Amen.
>
> *Romans 1:25*

The consequence of humanity's refusal to honour him as God is that
he "gave them up" to a variety of degrading practices, culminating in a
"debased mind" which leads finally to a long catalogue of sins. Idolatry—
wrong worship—is the root issue. When humans choose idolatry God

confirms our decision by withdrawing his protection. We come under the power of whatever we worship.

The history of the twentieth century is a testament to this truth. I remember standing in Red Square with a group of Russian students in the days of the Soviet Union, watching the soldiers guarding Lenin's tomb. I incautiously suggested this must be a boring job, whereupon one of the girls rebuked me: "éto svyatýnya" ("this is a holy place"). There was awe in her voice. Lenin was to be worshipped. People queued for hours to file past his embalmed corpse (with some of the old ladies reputedly crossing themselves), children in schools danced before images of him, the slogans on buildings proclaimed, "Lenin is with us." And the regime which he inaugurated went on to commit mass murder on an unprecedented scale and to build its economy on human sacrifice and slave labour. The greatest misery of the twentieth century occurred under the regimes which worshipped their leaders: Lenin, Stalin, Hitler,[39] Mao Zedong, Pol Pot, and so on. When we worship whatever is not God we make ourselves its slaves.

Jesus confronts and defeats these enslaving powers on the cross so that the divine project of true worship and shared rule over creation can go forward. To use the language of Galatians already quoted, we are "enslaved" to "the weak and worthless elementary principles of the world", but "For freedom Christ has set us free."[40]

Exodus is about freedom; we come now to the theme of Exile, which is about forgiveness.

The story of Israel: Exile

From the very beginning of her national life, Israel was prone to idolatry and sin. When Moses is on the mountain receiving the Law from the hand of God, Israel is already worshipping the Golden Calf on the plain below. In the desert they quickly fall to grumbling. Though there are some good times and some good leaders in Israel's history, the overall story is one of continuous falling into idolatrous worship of other gods, and all the sins which follow from that. As a result, the presence of God is eventually withdrawn from the people: the glory departs from the Temple, and the nation goes into Exile in Babylon, as predicted as far back as Deuteronomy 28. After seventy years the Exile comes to an end and the remnant of Israel is restored to the Land. But the return is always problematic. The nation is still mostly under pagan domination, the rebuilt Temple is a disappointment, and the glory of the Lord does not return, even though the prophets assure the people that this will come to pass in due time. In an important sense, the Exile continues. Israel is back in the Land but the promises of God are far from fulfilment. The story of Israel looks like a story in search of an ending.

While Exodus is about freedom from slavery, Exile tells us that Israel needs her sins forgiven. Israel abused her freedom and fell into idolatry and sin. She became incapable of fulfilling the divine calling to be the vehicle for the salvation of the world. She had become subject again to the powers that spoil human life, and could only be rescued from her plight if her sins could be forgiven.

The two themes—freedom and forgiveness—fit perfectly together in the larger context of the verse from Colossians 2 quoted earlier:

> And you, who were dead in your trespasses and the uncircumcision of your flesh, God made alive together with him, having forgiven us all our trespasses, by cancelling the record of debt that stood against us with its legal demands. This he set aside, nailing it to the cross. He disarmed the rulers and authorities and put them to open shame, by triumphing over them in him.
>
> *Colossians 2:13–15*

Paul is saying that the forgiveness of sins is the means whereby freedom from the powers is secured.

The link between Exodus and Exile, freedom and forgiveness, goes back to Jesus himself. It is Jesus himself who at the Last Supper brings together the two themes. He chooses the Exodus celebration of Passover to speak of the renewal of the covenant and the forgiveness of sins achieved through the shedding of his blood:

" . . . this is my blood of the covenant, which is poured out for
many for the forgiveness of sins."

Matthew 26:28

"This cup is the new covenant in my blood."

1 Corinthians 11:25

In the story of Israel's scriptures, the forgiveness of sins and the renewal
of covenant are the means of achieving the end of Exile:

Behold, the days are coming, declares the Lord, when I will make
a new covenant with the house of Israel and the house of Judah
. . . For I will forgive their iniquity, and I will remember their
sin no more.

Jeremiah 31:31, 34

The punishment of your iniquity, O daughter of Zion, is
accomplished; he will keep you in exile no longer . . .

Lamentations 4:22

The prophets are looking forward to the end of Exile, to a time when
Israel will no longer routinely go after other gods and fall into sin.

Just as the Exodus theme of freedom is evident in Jesus' ministry to
those afflicted by enslaving powers, including demonic powers, so also
the Exile theme of the forgiveness of sins is evident in his *declarations* of
forgiveness to sinners and his *demonstrations* of forgiveness in sharing
meals with sinners. To those with ears to hear these things would speak
of the end of Exile. Their experience, and the experience of generations of
Jews before them, was that the Exile had ended in the strict geographical
sense, but the prophetic promises of the return of YHWH to his Temple,
and the renewal of national life which would follow, had not happened.
Now Jesus is telling them in word and deed that the great promises are
finally to be fulfilled. Freedom and forgiveness are on their way. The
story which has been in search of an ending will, at last, get the ending
it deserves.

Just as we needed to understand something of the mechanism whereby the non-human powers operate through human authorities, so we also need some understanding of the mechanism whereby forgiveness brings freedom.

Sin and slavery

Sin enslaves us by subjecting us to the power of the things we worship. If you worship money, sex, or power, you become their slave. If you give your time, your energy, and your heart to any of these things, you forfeit your freedom and find yourself dominated by powers that are increasingly beyond your control. If, however, you repent of your sins and receive forgiveness, then the powers lose their power and freedom becomes a real possibility again.

The same pattern holds good not only for receiving forgiveness but for extending it to others. When you forgive someone, you are set free. As I write this, news has come through of the death of Jill Saward, who was the victim of a violent robbery and rape at Ealing Vicarage in London in 1986. In an interview in 2006, she said:

> Of course, sometimes I thought it might be quite nice to be full
> of hatred and revenge. But I think it creates a barrier and you're
> the one who gets damaged in the end. So, although it makes you
> vulnerable, forgiving is actually a release. I don't think I'd be here
> today without my Christian faith. That's what got me through.[41]

The covenant of vocation

The emphasis of this chapter has been on understanding the cross through the lens of Israel's scriptures, on the necessity of reading the story of the cross as part of the story to which it truly belongs and within which, alone, it makes full sense. Tom Wright has a helpful way of explaining something of the difference between the right story and another story which is similar but not quite the right one. He describes the commission given to humanity in Genesis 1 to have dominion as the "covenant of vocation". God gave a vocation to humanity and it is that vocation on which humanity has turned its back by refusing to worship him as God. The restoration and implementation of that vocation is what God is interested in. This is one of the central themes which Paul expounds in Romans 5 and Romans 8, as we saw in the previous chapter. When the Book of Revelation celebrates the victory of the cross, it immediately celebrates the restoration of humanity's capacity to reign:

> And they sang a new song, saying,
> "Worthy are you to take the scroll
>   and to open its seals,
> for you were slain, and by your blood you ransomed people for God
>   from every tribe and language and people and nation,
> and you have made them a kingdom and priests to our God,
>   and they shall *reign* on the earth."
>
> ### Revelation 5:9–10 (my italics)

When the great consummation arrives at the end of the book (that is, when heaven comes to earth), the covenant of vocation is fulfilled in the restoration of human authority over creation:

> . . . they will reign forever and ever.
>
> ### Revelation 22:5

The works contract

There is, however, a rather different way of understanding the divine purpose and the human predicament which Tom Wright describes as the "works contract". It is this which tends to dominate much of the church's thinking about the cross:

> The "works contract" functions in the popular mind like this. God told his human creatures to keep a moral code; their continuing life in the Garden of Eden depended on their keeping that code perfectly. Failure would incur the punishment of death. This was then repeated in the case of Israel with a sharpened-up moral code, [the] Mosaic law . . . [H]owever, Jesus obeyed this moral law perfectly and in his death paid the penalty on behalf of the rest of the human race. The overarching arrangement (the "works contract") between God and humans remained the same, but Jesus had done what was required.[42]

The works contract makes sin the issue: it says that our problem is that we have broken God's commandments. The covenant of vocation makes idolatry the bigger issue: it says that we have turned away from the living God and chosen to worship substitutes which have led us ever deeper into sin. In one sense, the two are saying something rather similar: that sin is a big problem and needs to be dealt with. But the covenant of vocation sets the problem of sin within a different story, another and larger narrative. That larger narrative makes a difference.

One way of making the point is to remind ourselves that there are two creation accounts in the Bible. Genesis 1 describes the covenant of vocation; Genesis 2 shows God setting boundaries. But Chapter 1 comes before Chapter 2: restoring humanity to its true vocation is the overriding purpose, and dealing with sins finds its proper meaning within that overall purpose.

Our image of God

What is at stake is our image of God. Anybody who has tried to work with the image of a person on a computer screen knows that it's easy to pull the image out of shape. The features are still there (eyes, mouth, nose, ears, hair etc.), but they're distorted: the proper proportions have gone and been replaced by a face which is barely recognizable. Something like this happens when we set the problem of sin within the wrong story: the image of God is pulled out of shape and his relationship to us and purpose for us are distorted.

The covenant of vocation pictures our relationship with God as a partnership, even a friendship. C. S. Lewis often spoke of friends characteristically sitting side by side, intent on a shared interest or project, in contrast to lovers who would naturally be pictured sitting face to face, intent on each other. Both are relevant and appropriate to the biblical picture of how God and humans relate to each other. But it's worth dwelling for a moment on the picture of friendship.

Friendship with God

God has invited humans to have a share in running his creation project. We are invited into friendship with him. Adam and Eve had a friendship with God as He walked in the garden in the cool of the evening breeze. Scripture calls Abraham "the friend of God".[43] God speaks to Moses "as a man speaks to his friend".[44] Job speaks wistfully of a time "when the friendship of God was upon my tent".[45] Jesus himself picks up the friendship theme and applies it to his relationship with his disciples:

> You are my friends if you do what I command you. No longer do
> I call you servants, for the servant does not know what his master
> is doing; but I have called you friends, for all that I have heard
> from my Father I have made known to you.
>
> *John 15:14–15*

When he speaks of his Father's love for him and of the way they work together in partnership, he uses the word for love which is the love between friends—*phileo*:

> ... the Father loves [*philei*] the Son and shows him all that he
> himself is doing
>
> *John 5:20*

The Louvre Museum in Paris houses one of the oldest icons in the world. It dates from the sixth century and portrays Jesus alongside an Egyptian hermit named Abbot Mena(s), who was martyred for his faith in the early fourth century. The delightful thing about this icon is that it pictures Jesus with his arm round Mena; and it is Mena, rather than Jesus, who has his arm raised in blessing. And if you look closely you can see that there is something odd about Mena's left eye: it is looking at Jesus, while his right eye looks out towards the viewer. It is a beautiful illustration of how the friendship of Jesus enables his disciples to bless God's world.

Friends are involved together in shared plans and shared action. That is the picture evoked by the covenant of vocation.

God as policeman and judge

The works contract, by contrast, evokes a different picture. In that scenario, the focus shifts from the invitation to partnership to the requirement of keeping the rules. As a result, the works contract can suggest an image of God as policeman or judge. God *is* the Judge and *will* judge humans and their sin. But that is not his primary purpose. Like any good parent he puts in place boundaries, norms, and rules. But that is not the parent's principal objective. The parent wants to bless the child, to enable the child to grow and flourish, to fulfil its potential. The rules are a means to an end, not the end itself.

Some reflections

To conclude this chapter, I offer some thoughts on what difference this perspective on the *achievement* of the cross might make to the church's *proclamation* of the cross.

1. Sin

How do we proclaim the death of Christ for our sins to a culture which rejects the concept of sin? It is sometimes said that the church's proclamation of the cross is answering a question which people are not asking. Since, by and large, postmodern Western culture doesn't operate with a worldview which includes the understanding that we have transgressed the Law of God, surely proclaiming the cross as God's answer to the problem of our sin is bound to fall flat? Sometimes, in truth, I think it does.

The answer, however, is the same as it has always been: the cross needs to be applied to our sins with proper discernment as to how the message is relevant to a particular situation. If we simply talk about "sin" to a contemporary audience, we are likely to be heard as merely exhibiting the church's long-standing and hypocritical obsession with sex (hypocritical because church leaders are so often caught offending in this area).

Some examples from the New Testament where the charge of sin is appropriately targeted may illustrate the point:

1. When Peter preaches to the crowd gathered at Pentecost, he focuses on their involvement in the crucifixion:

   . . . this Jesus whom you crucified.

   Acts 2:23, 36

   That is the point at which the accusation of sin hits home for them.
2. When Jesus gets into conversation with the Samaritan woman in John 4 he quickly homes in on her mixed-up marital history. He does it with consummate gentleness and kindness, but also with

perfect directness and candour. She gets the message very quickly and goes to share the news with her community.

3. When Paul preaches to the intellectuals of Athens, he focuses on idolatry:

> ... we ought not to think that the divine being is like gold or silver or stone, an image formed by the art and imagination of man. The times of ignorance God overlooked, but now he commands all people everywhere to repent.
>
> *Acts 17:29-30*

This focus on idolatry seems to have been a common theme in Paul's preaching to pagans. At Lystra he says to the people who are about to offer sacrifice to himself and Barnabas:

> ... why are you doing these things? We also are men, of like nature with you, and we bring you good news, that you should turn from these vain things to a living God, who made the heaven and the earth and the sea and all that is in them.
>
> *Acts 14:15*

He reminds the Thessalonians:

> ... how you turned to God from idols to serve the living and true God.
>
> *1 Thessalonians 1:9*

He tells the Colossians:

> Put to death therefore what is earthly in you: sexual immorality, impurity, passion, evil desire, and covetousness, which is idolatry.
>
> *Colossians 3:5*

The issue of who or what we worship is a very live issue today and may therefore offer one of the most relevant and powerful ways of preaching the cross. Spirituality—in the sense of what gives meaning to life and what we give our lives to—is very much *in*. Money, sex, and power are as seductive and powerful as ever, and the destructive consequences of putting them at the centre of our lives are not hard to illustrate.

The essential point is that we need to listen closely to the Holy Spirit for discernment about how we should speak about sin in any given situation. We may find that the sins that trouble people's consciences are not what we expect. It is the Holy Spirit who convicts the world of sin, righteousness, and judgement,[46] and presumably we make his task simpler if our message hits the right spot from the start.

I recently heard a vicar speak of being asked to visit a woman who was terminally ill in hospital. The family were not believers but were looking for comfort in a desperate situation. Sitting by her bedside, he chatted with her in a friendly way for a time about herself and her family, and then asked if there was any question she had for him. She replied that she was feeling very guilty because the lung cancer which put her in hospital was the result of her smoking. She felt she had let her family down, particularly her children. The vicar's immediate thought was to say that it really wasn't her fault but he was checked by a strong sense that the Holy Spirit was telling him to invite her to repent and receive forgiveness. He did just that, and she was immediately filled with a glorious sense of peace. Her husband was astonished by the immediate and visible change in his wife.

2. Creation

Our culture has become much more sensitive than previous generations about how we treat the environment. The cross has something to say about that:

> . . . in him all the fullness of God was pleased to dwell, and through him to reconcile to himself all things, whether on earth or in heaven, making peace by the blood of his cross.
>
> *Colossians 1:19–20*

The gospel is about the healing and reconciliation of the whole creation. God intends to restore to his world his peace, his shalom, so that it can flourish as intended. Centrally, that involves reconciling us who are God's appointed vicegerents over creation, but it is vital to make clear that the story is bigger than just us. Salvation is not only personal and focused on humans; it is cosmic. This is one aspect of the good news of the Kingdom which should resonate easily with our culture.

3. Freedom

Freedom has been and continues to be one of the watchwords of the twentieth and twenty-first centuries. Rightly so, if this chapter's analysis of the meaning of the cross is correct. Freedom is the heart of God for his children. We strive for it on many different fronts, and yet it so often proves very elusive. To present the cross as the definitive act of liberation brings together the heart of God and the longing of the human heart.

There are many ways this could be illustrated. For instance, when Paul talks to the Colossians in the passage already quoted in this chapter about covetousness, he equates it with idolatry. Covetousness is about much more than wanting more of something than you need or is good for you. It stems from putting second things first, from displacing God from his rightful place in our hearts. It is one of the chief sins of our day and it leads to addiction. We live in an age of rampant addiction: the headline-grabbing addictions of drugs, violence, paedophilia, pornography, and so on, and the everyday addictions of shopping, overeating, and social media. We long for the solution to all these issues but struggle to find it. The deepest and fullest answer is the forgiveness and freedom which come to us through the cross.

4. Story

I have, in this chapter, discussed the meaning of the cross almost entirely in terms of story. I have said next to nothing about the various theories of atonement which have produced so much angst, anger, and division in the church down the ages. This is not because I think they don't matter but because I think it's timely and helpful to step back and look at the cross from a different place, which is actually one of the key standpoints of the scriptures themselves: the perspective and standpoint of story. There are several benefits from this tactic. In the first place, it reveals much about the meaning of the cross which is not always evident from the theories of atonement. And secondly, it points towards story as one of the most important means not only of understanding but also of proclaiming the cross. The church needs to proclaim the cross both *from within* the story of Israel, and particularly the story of Jesus himself as it's told in the Gospels, and *from beyond* the scriptures, by reference to the multitude of stories, both fictional and factual, which echo and illustrate the story of the cross. Good preachers have always done this; what this chapter offers is a more solidly based rationale for the practice.

CHAPTER 4

Commission

In the last chapter we explored the meaning of the cross from the standpoint of story: the story of Israel and the story of Jesus. The Kingdom of God is a story; it is—as has often been pointed out—"His Story". The story continues with the resurrection, to which we will return in the final chapter. But how does it progress beyond the climactic events of the cross and resurrection? Is that the end? By no means. The story continues with the continuing ministry of Jesus. Luke makes this point in his Prologue to the book of Acts:

> In the first book, O Theophilus, I have dealt with all that Jesus *began to do and teach*, until the day when he was taken up, after he had given commands through the Holy Spirit to the apostles whom he had chosen.
>
> *Acts 1:1-2 (my italics)*

The Gospel narrative was only the beginning of the ministry of Jesus. The story of the church is the story, not just of the disciples of Jesus, but of what Jesus himself is continuing to do and to teach. And that story continues to this day, a point which Luke makes by ending his account in Acts with Paul under house arrest in Rome but continuing unstoppably to proclaim Jesus and the Kingdom:

> He lived there two whole years at his own expense, and welcomed all who came to him, proclaiming the kingdom of God and

teaching about the Lord Jesus Christ with all boldness and
without hindrance.

Acts 28:30–31

The implication is that, whatever the world does to the church, whatever
obstacles are put in the way of the progress of the gospel, the story will
go forward, Jesus will continue his work.

Jesus continues his work

Sister Maria de Lourdes Martins Cruz is a Roman Catholic nun in
East Timor who experienced a personal commission from Jesus to
minister to the poor. In response to that commission she established
the Institute of Brothers and Sisters in Christ, with a specific mission to
serve the poor and oppressed. In 1999, the people of East Timor voted
overwhelmingly for independence from Indonesia. The response of the
Indonesian military was to unleash a wave of violence and terror which
left large numbers of people homeless and destitute. Fifteen thousand of
them gathered in the forest around Sister Lourdes' institute. She and her
associates had a small barrel of rice but it was not enough to feed fifteen
people, let alone fifteen thousand. So she got up early every morning to
pray and then proceeded to cook rice from her barrel. The rice in that
barrel lasted for three weeks, until the day an Australian-led international
peacekeeping force arrived.[47]

To be faithful to Jesus, the church needs to be equipped to do as well
as to teach.

Doing and teaching

The doing and the teaching are both important, but it may be significant that Luke's Prologue to Acts puts doing before teaching. It is what Jesus *did*, as much as what he taught, which has changed the world. His practice of spending time with the despised and the marginalized, with women, children, tax collectors, prostitutes, and lepers, was at least as important as his actual teaching in communicating the revolutionary doctrine that all human beings are of equal value in the sight of God.

When people wanted to know more about Jesus, they were invited to "come and see"[48]—not just to come and listen to what he was saying, but to come and see what he was doing. Seeing and hearing belong together: first Jesus and then his disciples (and even Jesus' opponents) appeal on several occasions to this double experience of his ministry.[49] When Peter preaches the gospel to the household of Cornelius he describes Jesus' ministry as going about "*doing* good".[50]

So what exactly did Jesus expect his disciples to do? In John's Gospel he tells the disciples:

> As the Father has sent me, even so I am sending you.
>
> *John 20:21*

There is a parallelism between the mission of the Son and the mission of the church: the one is a continuation of the other. And just in case it is suggested that this commission applies only to the apostles, the same Gospel is clear that it encompasses all those who believe in Jesus:

> Truly, truly, I say to you, whoever believes in me will also do the works that I do; and greater works than these will he do, because I am going to the Father.
>
> *John 14:12*

Luke's Gospel ends with Jesus telling the disciples that repentance and forgiveness are to be proclaimed to all nations, and they are to wait for the power of God to come upon them for this purpose. Mark appears to end rather inconclusively, perhaps with its original ending lost and a later addition stuck on instead. But the later addition, if that is what it is, expects the disciples to launch a world-wide mission.

The Great Commission

The most highly-developed form of the commission is found at the end of Matthew's Gospel:

> All authority in heaven and on earth has been given to me. Go therefore and make disciples of all nations, baptizing them in the name of the Father and of the Son and of the Holy Spirit, teaching them to observe all that I have commanded you. And behold, I am with you always, to the end of the age.
>
> *Matthew 28:18–20*

The commission is to make disciples. That is, Jesus is telling the existing disciples to bring other people into the same relationship to himself which they have discovered. They are to lead others to repentance and faith and to a lifelong commitment to knowing and following Jesus.

The commission is striking in its universality:

1. It flows from the universal authority of Jesus: *all authority in heaven and on earth* now belongs to him.
2. It is universal in its reach: *all nations* are the object of the church's mission.
3. It is universal in scope, embracing (literally translated) *"all things whatsoever that I have commanded you"*. This, of course, includes the command to make disciples, and therefore implies that the creation of new disciples is a rolling programme, a relay race in which one generation passes on the baton of disciple-making to the next.
4. It is universal in time, encompassing (again, literally translated) *all the days* until the new creation comes in its fullness.

Confidence in the gospel

Jesus' words are designed to sustain the disciples' confidence in the gospel. Some were doubting even as Jesus was talking to them.[51] The church has had to wrestle with doubts about the universality of the gospel ever since. These are just some of the challenges involved:

1. The universal authority of Jesus is challenged by the continuing reality of evil and suffering in the world, by the recurrent failures of his followers, and by rival claims to authority—religious, scientific, political, or philosophical.

2. The universal reach of the gospel is challenged by atheistic regimes which want to keep God out of people's lives, by the desire to protect and preserve culture (one's own or other people's), by the discovery—particularly in the last two hundred years or so—of the sheer plurality and diversity of human experience and human religiosity, by the postmodern distrust of universal truth claims.

3. The universal scope of the gospel as embracing all the commandments of Jesus is challenged by the fact that obedience demands faith, a willingness to suffer, to take risks, and to face failure.

4. The universal extent of the commission in time is challenged by the belief of some Christians that the commands of Jesus to do miraculous things ceased to apply after the apostolic age, and by the lapse of two thousand years since the original events: when *is* the end of the age going to arrive? It seems a very long time coming—isn't all this stuff past its sell-by date?

In the face of all these challenges, the church is called to keep its nerve, to continue—humbly but boldly and persistently—seeking to be obedient to Jesus. The word translated "observe" means to keep, hold, or follow. The whole commission is meant to be held on to in its holistic entirety, without letting anything fall into neglect or disuse.

Training for disciples

If this is to be a reality, then a key task of the church is training. Matthew's Gospel is constructed precisely with this agenda in mind. We will now explore some key moments in Jesus' training of the disciples.

The story of the healing of the paralytic brought to Jesus by his friends features in all three Synoptic Gospels. Mark's version, which according to the usual scholarly consensus was the first Gospel to be written, concludes:

> . . . they were all amazed and glorified God, saying, "We never saw anything like this!"
>
> *Mark 2:12*

Matthew tells essentially the same story but his conclusion is different:

> When the crowds saw it, they were filled with awe, and they glorified God, *who had given such authority to human beings.*
>
> *Matthew 9:8, NRSV (my italics)*

Matthew has shaped his version of the story to launch the idea that Jesus is not simply healing physical conditions; he is showing what can be done by humans whose authority over God's world has been restored to what it should be. Jesus is modelling what his followers will learn to do. In the background is the divine mandate to humans in Genesis 1:26–28 to rule over his creation. This was severely compromised by the sin of Adam, so that the creation no longer responds to human authority as it was meant to, and humans no longer rule with the respect and care for God's creation that they were meant to exercise. However, all this is going to be put right through the arrival of the Kingdom of God. When God's rightful rule is restored the rightful rule of humans under his lordship will be restored too.

At the end of Chapter 9, Matthew summarizes what Jesus has been doing up to this point:

> And Jesus went throughout all the cities and villages, teaching in
> their synagogues and proclaiming the gospel of the kingdom and
> healing every disease and every affliction . . . And he called to him
> his twelve disciples and gave them authority over unclean spirits,
> to cast them out, and to heal every disease and every affliction.
>
> *Matthew 9:35,10:1*

The disciples are sent out by Jesus to do what he is doing. The wording is
the same in both the summary of Jesus' ministry and the commission he
gives to his disciples: they are to heal "every disease and every affliction".
What Jesus does and what he commands his disciples to do are the same.

Feeding the five thousand

In Chapter 14 Matthew recounts the feeding of the five thousand. Jesus
refuses to send the hungry crowds home as the disciples want him to; he
tells them to do something about the situation:

> . . . *you* give them something to eat.
>
> *Matthew 14:16 (my italics)*

They protest that they don't have the resources for that, so Jesus tells
them to give what they have to him. He gets the crowds to sit down,
gives thanks, and passes the food to the disciples to distribute. He needs
their help; he could hardly make his way round a crowd of over 5,000
people personally handing out bread and fish. But involving the disciples
in the distribution is more than a matter of practical necessity. They are
helping not only with the practicalities of getting the food out, but with
the miraculous multiplication itself. The bread and fish multiply in their
hands. They don't keep trotting back to Jesus for a top-up. As they put
food into people's hands they find that it keeps coming, just as Sister
Lourdes and her nuns discovered; it doesn't run out until everybody has

been fed. They are learning what it feels like to do the things that Jesus does.

Walking on water

After the feeding of the five thousand Jesus sends the disciples away to the other side of the lake while he goes up the mountain to pray. The disciples have a rough time in the boat battling the weather. Eventually Jesus comes to them, walking on the water. Their first reaction is fear, but Jesus reassures them that it really is him. Peter responds:

> Lord, if it is you, command me to come to you on the water.
>
> *Matthew 14:28*

Peter is quite tentative, unsure whether this is Jesus or not. But he is beginning to realize that, whatever Jesus does, he, Peter, should be doing too. He has seen enough of how Jesus involves his disciples in his ministry and coaxes them into imitating himself to expect that the same pattern is going to be repeated now. So he decides to test things out. If this really is Jesus, then Jesus will do what he always does: tell him to get involved. He asks: "Lord, if it is you . . . ". Jesus replies simply: "Come." Peter obeys, and finds that he can walk on water, even if only briefly. He learns something more about replicating the ministry of Jesus, including the fact that it will sometimes involve failure.

Facing up to failure

Facing up to failure is a feature of the Gospel accounts of healing the sick. In Matthew 17, the last occasion when the disciples are involved in healing the sick in this Gospel, a man approaches Jesus and reports that the disciples have failed to heal his epileptic son. Jesus is exasperated by their lack of faith:

> O faithless and twisted generation, how long am I to be with you?
> How long am I to bear with you? Bring him here to me.
>
> ***Matthew 17:17***

The question of faith looms large in Jesus' training of the disciples. Among the Gospel writers, it is Matthew who specially emphasizes faith. In this Gospel, Jesus rebukes the disciples five times for their "little faith",[52] a phrase which occurs only once in the rest of the New Testament.[53] Lack of faith seems to be the thing that most disappoints him. Lack of faith prevents him from doing "many mighty works" in his home town of Nazareth.[54]

The importance of faith

Jesus looks for faith and commends it warmly when he finds it. Sometimes he finds it in the person who comes seeking his help, as for instance with the woman with the discharge of blood, and the two blind men in Matthew 9. Sometimes he finds it in those who seek healing for a friend, a family member, or a servant, as for instance with the healing of the centurion's servant in Matthew 8 and the healing of the paralytic in Matthew 9. Sometimes it is Jesus' own faith which has to suffice, as in the passage just quoted where the disciples fail to heal an epileptic boy and Jesus steps in to get the job done.

Jesus is keenly attuned to the presence or absence of faith in his hearers and makes a point of exposing what is going on under the surface. He frequently rebukes unbelief. He rebukes the scribes for their attitude to his ministry to the paralytic let down through the roof by his friends.

An instructive case study in the importance Jesus attaches to faith can be found in the healing of a blind man from the village of Bethsaida recorded in Mark 8:22–26. First, he takes the man out of the village. Second, he not only spits on his eyes but lays hands on him as well. Third, Jesus takes two goes to get the healing complete. Finally, once the job is done, he warns the man to go straight home without even entering the village. The implication is that in this case Jesus has to put in place special measures to get the healing done, and there may well be something toxic about the village which makes the job tough going even for Jesus. Why is that? Perhaps it is that Bethsaida had already rejected his ministry, and that rejection had set a tone of unbelief which severely limited anything more which could be done within its vicinity:

> Woe to you, Chorazin! Woe to you, Bethsaida! For if the mighty works done in you had been done in Tyre and Sidon, they would have repented long ago in sackcloth and ashes.
>
> *Matthew 11:21*

The church continues to heal the sick

After the Gospels, we find that the church continues to heal the sick. There are a number of healings recorded in the book of Acts. Paul likewise assumed that God would do works of power in the churches. Hence his inclusion of "gifts of healings" and "works of power" among the spiritual gifts listed in 1 Corinthians 12, where there is no suggestion that the gifts are limited to special people or accredited leaders or a particular time frame. In the same vein he casually refers (in the course of an argument about something else) to the "works of power" which God does among the Galatians:

> Does he who supplies the Spirit to you and works miracles
> [literally, "powerful things"] among you do so by works of the
> law, or by hearing with faith?
>
> *Galatians 3:5*

For him and for them, this was normal—something to be expected as part of the life of the Christian community.

The language we use

Living up to Jesus' expectations of faith feels, at least in the affluent West, like a big ask. I think part of our difficulty is the language we use. We call these things "supernatural". And therein lies a problem. We need for a moment to take a step back and explore again the theology which underlies the New Testament expectation of works of power.

The Kingdom of God involves restoring to humanity its capacity to exercise godly dominion over created things. The power and authority of God himself have been delegated to us. They are therefore meant to flow through us as a *natural* part of who we are and how we operate. As we know, things now don't work as they should because of the invasion of sin into God's creation. There is a split between heaven and earth which the Kingdom comes to heal. That is one reason why Matthew nearly always (alone among the evangelists) speaks of the "Kingdom of Heaven" rather than the "Kingdom of God". "Heaven" is, of course, a reverent Jewish way of speaking about God, but I suspect Matthew is saying something more important and interesting than that. He is telling us that the essence of the Kingdom is the life of heaven once again united with life on earth so that the two function in full harmony with each other. The rule of Heaven is restored to earth. This is the *natural* condition of human beings; our present condition is not natural: it is sub-natural.

When we use language which opposes what is "natural" to what is "supernatural" we obscure this crucial understanding of the purpose of God in giving us the Kingdom, of what is truly natural to us—what accords with our essential created nature. It would be more accurate and more enlightening to use the biblical terminology of "heaven" and "earth" rather than "natural" and "supernatural". "Natural" and "supernatural" suggest things which don't belong together and can only come together in exceptional circumstances. But in the Kingdom heaven and earth are being brought back together because together is where they belong.

Think back to the experience of the disciples assisting Jesus in the feeding of the five thousand. The food multiplied in their hands. I suggest the experience was at one level entirely ordinary and unemotional. I don't think it was at all like some of the portrayals of Jesus on film where he has to screw himself up to a high pitch of desperate intensity to make the thing happen. In the Gospel accounts, by contrast, he simply gives thanks to God and proceeds to hand out the food, and the disciples just get involved and get on with the job. They are learning what it means to do works of power, to live on earth with the resources of heaven. We will return to this again in Chapter 8.

Why focus on healing?

I have said a good deal so far about the issue of healing. Following Jesus involves many other things besides healing, including many things which will be unremarkable and go unnoticed except by God himself. I have chosen to focus particularly on healing because:

1. Healing is a sign of the Kingdom and of the new creation: it points to the presence of the Kingdom today and forward to the consummation of the Kingdom at the End, when all things are made new. As such, it should be a permanent part of the church's ministry as a vital witness to the purpose of God.
2. Healing is very prominent in the Gospels: some estimates suggest 25% of the narrative is taken up with physical healing. It has been said of Mark's Gospel that Jesus is always either *healing* somebody,

or on his way *from* healing somebody, or on his way *to* healing somebody.

3. Healing highlights the issue of faith in a very pointed way.
4. Healing illustrates most of the theological and practical questions involved in seeking to emulate the ministry of Jesus.
5. Healing is (naturally enough) still controversial in the church, whereas many of the other things Jesus did, such as rebuking injustice, prioritizing the poor and marginalized, and so on, are not. I think the issues underlying the controversy are worth airing.

I want now to address some of the practical issues which arise when we embark on seeking to heal the sick.

Heal the sick

What are we actually doing? Jesus commanded his disciples to "heal the sick".[55] He didn't tell them to pray for the sick. There is much more in the New Testament about healing the sick than there is about praying for them. We need to do both. The problem is that praying for the sick ("Lord, please heal this man's painful back") is easier than healing the sick ("In the name of Jesus, get up and walk"). Jesus addressed people and conditions rather than petitioning God: he told lame people to get up and he commanded blind eyes to see and deaf ears to be unstopped. All the evidence says that he meant his disciples to do the same. When Peter and John met a lame man at the Beautiful Gate of the Temple, Peter commanded him:

> In the name of Jesus Christ of Nazareth, rise up and walk!
>
> *Acts 3:6*

Healing the sick in this way is one element in the restoration of humanity's rule over creation. We are learning to exercise the authority and power of the Kingdom over all that spoils the work of God. It takes some getting used to and it's easy to lapse back into the mode of petitionary prayer. And often it is easier to use the language of "praying for the sick" (as I have done in this chapter) than to labour the point about "healing" the sick. But if we want to be faithful to Jesus we should be learning to exercise authority over sickness.

It's important to point out (although this is not the subject of this chapter) that we seek to exercise authority over sickness *both* through medicine *and* through the exercise of spiritual power and authority. The two work very well together.

When it doesn't work

What do we do when it doesn't work? We have seen that the experience of the disciples in the Gospels included failure, and even Jesus was limited by lack of faith. What do we do? Faced with the difficulties and disappointments which are endemic to exercising a ministry of healing, people have often resorted to two explanations for the times when healing is not forthcoming:

1. This person has not been healed because God is working some deeper good in them through their pain.
2. This person has not been healed because now is not the right time, though they may be healed at another time.

The ministry of Jesus gives the lie to both those ideas: he never told anybody that their pain was good for them and he never told anybody to come again another day.[56] If we truly believed that someone was not healed because God was doing them good through their pain, or that now was not the time for them to be healed, we could never suggest they see a doctor. If God is doing you good through your pain, you had better put up with it![57] Many people bear chronic pain with extraordinary courage and faith and grow in patience through the experience. But recognizing that is not the same as saying that the pain was God's intention for them.

We are assured by Paul that all things work together for good for those who love God, but that does not mean that all things are good things.

Sickness was not eradicated in the New Testament church. We are living in the overlap between this present age and the age to come. The age to come has burst in upon this present age and made available the powers of the age to come, but this present age still exerts a powerful influence. In particular, death is still a fact of life:

> The *last enemy to be destroyed* is death.
>
> **1 Corinthians 15:26 (my italics)**

We're not there yet, and until we are, our experience of the powers of the age to come will be incomplete. They are, after all, the powers of the age *to come*.

Disappointment

Given that not everybody is healed, isn't it kinder to leave the sick person sick rather than risk the disappointment of not getting healed? In my experience, it depends how you approach things. It's best not to promise healing, because if it doesn't materialize then somebody has to take the blame. It is imperative never to suggest that the person being prayed for has failed through their lack of faith. Jesus blamed the disciples when things didn't work, never the patient. If blame is required it must always fall on the person ministering rather than the one ministered to. When healing doesn't happen, it's fine to offer to pray on another occasion and as often as the person is willing to keep going, if necessary. I remember praying unsuccessfully for the blind eye of an elderly lady regularly week by week for some considerable time. She had a lot more faith than I did and persisted in asking for prayer at our midweek communion service—until eventually she died. I think the simple fact of receiving prayer was comforting to her. Where the gift of healing is exercised with love and kindness, the person is blessed by God and knows they have met with him even if they don't exactly get what they wanted.

Good news for the poor

The gospel is specifically good news to the poor; they are the natural heirs of the Kingdom, the ones who most easily receive it with rich and simple faith. The faith exhibited by the poor is one of the ways God releases his Kingdom, one of the ways he restores justice and rights the wrongs in his world:

> . . . has not God chosen those who are poor in the world to be rich in faith and heirs of the kingdom, which he has promised to those who love him?
>
> *James 2:5*

In the affluent West there is often not much faith, and the amount of healing experienced will be correspondingly limited and patchy. Travel to rural Africa, on the other hand, or any other place where modern medicine is either impossibly expensive or simply not available, and you will likely see healing flow much more easily. I remember praying for a man's deaf ear in Kenya and asking him if anything had changed—had his hearing improved? He looked at me in wide-eyed surprise: yes, of course it had, he could hear perfectly—what did I expect?

The object of our faith

What are we putting our faith in? Is it faith in God or faith in our faith? Faith is essentially about looking away from ourselves to God. However, emphasizing the importance of faith can easily lead to an anxious and destructive introspection: examining our faith to assess its strength rather than turning to God.

The great nineteenth-century pioneer missionary to China, James Hudson Taylor, wrestled deeply with this issue. A significant moment of personal revelation was given to him in the year 1870:

> It was just in his usual reading, as he often related, that he was struck with the words, "*Ekete pistin Theou*". How strangely new they seemed! "Have (or hold) the faithfulness of God": surely it was a passage he had never seen before? Turning to the corresponding words in English he read (Mark 11.22): "Have faith in God". Ah, that was familiar enough; and something within him whispered, "the old difficulty!" How gladly would he have an increase in faith in God, if only he knew how! But this seemed entirely different. It laid the emphasis on another side of the matter in a way he found surprisingly helpful. It was not 'have' in your own heart and mind, however you can get it, "faith in God", but simply "hold fast, count upon *His faithfulness*."[58]

Hudson Taylor's translation of the Greek word *pistis* in this context is exactly parallel to the fresh translation in Romans 3, Galatians 2, and Galatians 3 which we explored in Chapter 2. There the phrase in question was "the faithfulness of *Jesus*"; here it is "the faithfulness of *God*". The point is the same: by reading the text in this way we are encouraged to look away from ourselves to God/Jesus. We are exercising faith, not in faith, but in God himself.

For Hudson Taylor this was no mere theory. Time after time he proved the faithfulness of God in extraordinary answers to prayer for the provision of personnel and funds to evangelize the unreached millions of inland China. He grasped the key lesson that discipleship is learning to live on earth with the resources of heaven. And true to the commission of Jesus, he passed on that lesson to countless others.

The New Testament, taken as a whole, encourages us to believe that we could see a lot more of the power of God released in us and through us than we do. Perseverance is key. The more we expect God to work, and the more we act on that expectation—the more risks we are willing to take—the more we will see the Kingdom come.

Some reflections

Now for some reflections on the implications of Jesus' commission to make disciples.

1. Confidence

Jesus' final commission calls for confidence in him and in his gospel. In a pluralistic, postmodern, multi-ethnic, multi-faith, and generally affluent society, that is demanding. It runs counter to everything that most people take for granted. It flies in the face of what the media and the intelligentsia proclaim with almost every breath/sentence/tweet/post. It is the job of theologians to confront that barrage of confidence-sapping material and enable the church to hold fast to the word of Jesus. Not by ignoring the issues or just shouting louder, but by patient, prayerful, and thoughtful engagement. I have not often (ever?) heard the intercessions on Sunday pray for theologians, but I think it would be good if they did.

2. Nurture

I have highlighted the focus of Jesus on training his disciples. He spent three years modelling his ministry with a small group of people and gradually involving them in it. This, I suggest, is what he had in mind when he told us to make disciples—a substantial period of induction and training in the things of God which enables new believers to stand on their own feet, and live out their faith with the ability to meet the challenges which come their way. The church has sometimes been quite good at making converts—getting people to a place of repentance and faith. It has not always been as good at making disciples. Recent years have seen a revival of interest in the ancient practice of the catechumenate, and various "Beta courses" have been produced which seek to take new believers beyond "Alpha" or whatever else has been their way in to faith. But I don't think the church as a whole has yet grasped how important this is; it's time we gave much more attention to such a vital issue. We need to develop a church culture where the routine expectation is that new believers will automatically become part of a substantial and fairly prolonged period of nurture.

3. Faith

We have seen that faith was important to Jesus: he commended its presence, rebuked and was constrained by its absence, and in the case of at least one healing encounter took considerable trouble to avoid a location which was associated with unbelief. We might wonder why this is so. Surely God is not dependent on our faith or lack of it to do what he wants to do? In one sense this is obviously the case. I think the issue goes back to the divine commission in Genesis 1, that humans should share in God's rule over creation. He chooses to honour that original commission and not to override our refusal to share the government with him. He invites our friendship and cooperation. But if we want to do things on our own and in our own way he will leave us to it. Adam and Eve chose to mistrust God and believe the serpent; restoring the relationship entails learning to trust again.

We need to grow in faith. We will probably often need to pray "I believe; help my unbelief!"[59] That means, among other things, that we need to commit to believing God rather than our own experience. If we live only by what we see happen, we will never grow in faith. Our experience will be self-limiting. Most people who see God do amazing things go through times when he appears not to be listening; but they persevere anyway. Not, of course, that we should pretend that something has happened when it hasn't. We will need to be ruthlessly truthful and realistic in assessing these things.

The issue of faith concerns not just individuals but gatherings and communities—this is a crucial lesson of the ministry of Jesus. A gathering of "believers" who don't believe will see much less of the power of God than a gathering where faith is real. Churches have a responsibility to grow in faith and put to death the cynicism and scepticism which are so often endemic among us. I have seen a Christian leader graciously, politely, and with a smile invite the sceptics in a congregation to disappear to the church hall for coffee before he embarked on modelling healing ministry. To repeat: this is not about encouraging people to be gullible, but it is a call to serious engagement with the purpose of God, to be a participant and not just a spectator.

4. Language

I have suggested that the language of "natural" versus "supernatural" is not helpful if we are trying to live the life of the Kingdom. If the Kingdom is about heaven invading earth, then it is not appropriate to set the two in opposition to each other. Jesus came to reconcile us to God, which means the long-standing divorce between the two spheres of God's one creation is coming to an end. It is often said that Christians should be "naturally supernatural and supernaturally natural". That is a way of saying that the two spheres really belong together and should not be separated. I wonder if we could acknowledge that and get rid of the words entirely. I wonder if "natural" and "supernatural" are terms which owe more to Greek philosophy than to a biblically inspired theology. The Bible talks about heaven and earth, flesh and spirit, power and weakness. Perhaps there are theologians somewhere with the appropriate philosophical understanding who can help us out.

CHAPTER 5

Character

In the previous chapter we began to explore the Great Commission of Jesus to make disciples. We focused on Jesus training his disciples to do the same kinds of things that he did: heal the sick, feed the hungry, and so on. This training had a dual focus: it was important that disciples should learn to do what Jesus did, because only in that way could they continue to be channels for the Kingdom to come on earth as in heaven; but beyond that, they were being trained for an even bigger purpose—for the day when the Kingdom would come in its fullness, and humanity would be properly restored to its original purpose of sharing the divine government of the universe. They were being trained to rule.

Character training

But discipleship involves more than being trained to *do* something. It also—and equally importantly—involves training to *be* something, to become a certain kind of person, the kind of person who is beginning to exhibit the characteristics outlined by Jesus in the Sermon on the Mount. Being and doing belong together, and if the task of becoming the person we were meant to be is neglected, then the doing quite quickly becomes toxic. Gifted and powerful people can sometimes use their gifts not to bless and empower but to dominate and control.

The issue of character is urgent for the church in the Western world. All too often the life and ministry of leaders in the church implode as they succumb to the temptations of (usually) money, sex, or power. And the problem is certainly not confined to leaders. The statistics on divorce, suggesting that churchgoers are no better at sustaining a healthy marriage than the rest of the population, are a clear indication that issues of character are not being adequately addressed amongst us. We are falling a long way short of Jesus' call to be "perfect";[60] it's almost as if we've given up trying.

There are probably many reasons why this is the case. I want to tackle only what I believe is the underlying theological issue.[61] This can be simply stated as follows: it's about the goal of the Christian life. Is the goal to make it to heaven when we die, and there forever enjoy rest, happiness, and the presence of God? If that is the goal, then it's not immediately clear what might be the purpose of our life now, beyond perhaps ensuring that we don't make such a mess of things that we endanger our salvation, and that we share our faith so that others can get to heaven too. The discontinuity between that conception of the future and our life on earth in the present makes it hard to see how the two are meant to be related.

Preparation for the future

If, however, the goal is to share in the divine government of a renewed cosmos, then this life takes on new meaning as the preparation and training ground for that great vision. The kind of person we are, and are becoming, becomes a crucial issue. Discipleship becomes a project worth prioritizing. Seeking first the Kingdom of God looks like good sense.

Stephen Covey wrote that there are seven habits of highly effective people. Habit 2 is "Begin with the end in mind".[62] The New Testament calls us to "begin with the end in mind" by developing the kind of character which will fit us for the future God has in store for us.

There is an intriguing commentary from Jesus on his own (tricky to interpret) parable of the dishonest manager (Luke 16:1–9):

One who is faithful in a very little is also faithful in much, and one who is dishonest in a very little is also dishonest in much. If then you have not been faithful with the unrighteous wealth, who will entrust to you the true riches? And if you have not been faithful with that which is another's, who will give you that which is your own?

Luke 16:10–12

Jesus is contrasting "unrighteous wealth" which belongs to "another" with "true riches" which are "your own". He seems to be saying that our destiny is to be entrusted with handling riches which really are riches in a sense beyond our present experience, and that these riches will really belong to us. If we have become the kind of people who can be trusted with real wealth and trusted actually to own it, then this is what we will enter into. He is holding before us a vision of the future which will mean owning and administering the rich resources of the universe.

The link between developing character and this kind of future destiny comes to expression in Romans 5:

Therefore, since we have been justified by faith, we have peace with God through our Lord Jesus Christ. Through him we have also obtained access by faith into this grace in which we stand, and we rejoice in hope of the glory of God. Not only that, but we rejoice in our sufferings, knowing that suffering produces endurance, and endurance produces character, and character produces hope, and hope does not put us to shame, because God's love has been poured into our hearts through the Holy Spirit who has been given to us.

Romans 5:1–5

Character is a link in the chain which leads from justification to glory. We will begin with the question of glory and then come back to the question of character.

The glory of God

Justification, says Paul, means peace with God, a place to stand (the grace of God), and a purpose to hope for: the glory of God. The glory of God is the goal—the thing at which the whole enterprise of the gospel is aimed.

We saw in Chapter 2 that Paul's vision of glory includes as a central component the restoration of humanity's proper dominion over creation. In Romans 8 Paul has more to say about this goal of glorification and its place in the purpose of God:

> For those whom he [God] foreknew he also predestined to be conformed to the image of his Son, in order that he might be the firstborn among many brothers. And those whom he predestined he also called, and those whom he called he also justified, and those whom he justified he also glorified.
>
> *Romans 8:29–30*

It's easy to assume that being "conformed to the image of his Son" simply means acquiring the moral character of Jesus: his goodness, gentleness, patience, and so on. Of course, it includes that. But when Paul explores the image of God in Jesus more fully in Colossians, it becomes clear that this embraces his rule over creation:

> He is the image of the invisible God, the firstborn of all creation. For by him all things were created, in heaven and on earth, visible and invisible, whether thrones or dominions or rulers or authorities—all things were created through him and for him. And he is before all things, and in him all things hold together. And he is the head of the body, the church. He is the beginning, the firstborn from the dead, that in everything he might be pre-eminent.
>
> *Colossians 1:15–18*

Glorification in Romans has often been treated as a synonym for sanctification, as if the end point of the purpose of God was to make people holy. Glorification is bigger than that. Making people holy makes them fit to rule.

The development of character

We can now go back to the question of character. The Greek word (*dokimé*) means the process of testing something, and then the result of the testing: a tried and tested character. The same word turns up in Philippians 2:22, where Paul writes of Timothy's "proven worth". The clear implication is that the kind of character Paul is thinking of does not descend fully formed from heaven but is the result of a process.

This is reinforced by the fact that the preceding term in the chain leading from justification to glory is "endurance". The same word is usually translated "patience" in Romans 8:25 where the context, as in Romans 5, is a discussion of hope. It means something like "sticking it out"—keeping going without getting discouraged and without giving up. Again, a process—perhaps a long process—is clearly implied. And not just a long process, but almost certainly a process that in some respects is painful, since the term which comes before "endurance" is "suffering". The psychiatrist Dr Frank Lake liked to take apart the elements of the Greek word for endurance and translate it "sticking it out *under*". He was emphasizing that this kind of patience/endurance involves living under the pressure of some very difficult circumstances without giving up. The same train of thought—using some of the same words—shows up in James 1:12 (my translation):

> Blessed is the man who sticks it out under trial because, when he
> has passed the test, he will receive the crown of life, which God
> has promised to those who love him.

Thus Paul is able to speak of rejoicing in suffering because its final outcome is not despair but hope, a hope that does not disappoint "because God's love has been poured into our hearts through the Holy Spirit who has been given to us" (Romans 5:5).

The work of the Holy Spirit in the human heart is the guarantee that the process of character formation will go all the way and lead the Christian into the fruition of the hope set before us—the glory of God. Having given us his Holy Spirit, God is not going to give up on us short of the accomplished goal.

Divine-human interaction

At this point it should be becoming clear that the process of forming Christian character involves both God and us. We do not receive godly character as a package at conversion—it develops over time. We are asked to cooperate. Life will send us experiences of suffering which, in the providence of God, can be turned to good. In order for suffering to do its work in us, we will need to stick it out without giving up.

This idea of cooperating with God makes some Christians very anxious about detracting from the pure grace of God—as if we could contribute to our salvation and thus put God in our debt. It's important to note, before we leave Romans 5, that when Paul sets the scene in this passage, he places great emphasis on the grace of God. He speaks of "this grace in which we stand".[63] Grace is the ground on which we stand: the foundation of everything else, the presupposition on which all else depends. It is as basic to the whole process of progressing from justification to glory as the earth on which we stand is basic to our existence. In other words, whatever we do by way of cooperation with God is at the same time God himself working in and through us. It is not that God does some of the work and we do the rest; it means, rather, that both we and God are fully involved at every point.

This is a conundrum with which Paul wrestled in giving an account of the work of God in his own life:

> ... by the grace of God I am what I am, and his grace towards
> me was not in vain. On the contrary, I worked harder than any of
> them, though it was not I, but the grace of God that is with me.
>
> *1 Corinthians 15:10*

He acknowledges fully the primacy of grace, but makes it plain that grace was working *within* him rather than *apart* from him, and therefore he himself was totally involved all the time.

The other model which may cast some light on this issue is the interplay of divine and human authorship in scripture. Evangelical Christians (and it's usually evangelicals who get worried about diminishing the grace of God in this context) have often been happy to say that scripture is one hundred per cent the work of human authors and also one hundred per cent inspired by God. The same could be said of the formation of character. Human will and divine purpose are fully at play both in the formation of scripture and in the formation of character, and in each case the one does not diminish the other.

The new heart

We now need to explore how this interplay between divine and human action works in practice, beginning with the human heart.

Jeremiah said that "the heart is deceitful above all things, and desperately sick;"[64] in the same vein Jesus told the disciples:

> What comes out of a person is what defiles him. For from within,
> out of the heart of man, come evil thoughts, sexual immorality,
> theft, murder, adultery, coveting, wickedness, deceit, sensuality,
> envy, slander, pride, foolishness.
>
> *Mark 7:20–22*

As preachers have sometimes said, the heart of the problem is the problem of the heart. But Jeremiah prophesies that the new covenant will deal with the problem of the heart:

> . . . this is the covenant that I will make with the house of Israel after those days, declares the Lord: I will put my law within them, and I will write it on their hearts. And I will be their God, and they shall be my people.
>
> *Jeremiah 31:33*

Similarly, Ezekiel:

> I will give you a new heart, and a new spirit I will put within you. And I will remove the heart of stone from your flesh and give you a heart of flesh.
>
> *Ezekiel 36:26*

When the first Christian sermon was preached by Peter at Pentecost, the hearers were "cut to the heart".[65] Their hearts were changed. The ancient promise of Deuteronomy was fulfilled:

> . . . the Lord your God will circumcise your heart and the heart of your offspring, so that you will love the Lord your God with all your heart and with all your soul, that you may live.
>
> *Deuteronomy 30:6*

The project of Christian character formation is founded on a fundamental renewal of the heart. It is not a project of self-improvement or self-salvation; rather, it is the outworking of the heart's renewal to embrace the whole personality. At the deepest level, this gift from God releases new desires and new priorities. This new centre of the human personality is sometimes spoken of in the New Testament as the heart and sometimes as the spirit. As in the prophecy of Ezekiel 36, the two terms can be used interchangeably.

Because this is such a profound transformation, it can feel, particularly in the first flush of conversion, as if everything has changed—as if the whole person has been released from its past captivity to sin in its various forms. Indeed, some changes may be more or less instantaneous at conversion. But sooner or later it becomes clear that there is plenty of stuff which remains to be dealt with. The mistake which Christians have often made at this juncture is to go back to Jeremiah's lament over the deceitfulness of the human heart and apply it to themselves. That is a mistake. That way lies despair, for it makes it seem as if God really has done nothing much to change us, or else we have messed up so badly (or are such bad people) that even the grace of God cannot reach us. We need to be (re-)assured that the hard, deceitful heart has been replaced in the Christian believer by the new heart of flesh. What remains to be done—and it is no small thing—is to seek the sanctification of the whole personality, including the body:

> Now may the God of peace himself sanctify you completely, and may your whole spirit and soul and body be kept blameless at the coming of our Lord Jesus Christ.
>
> *1 Thessalonians 5:23*

The sanctification of the body

We may wonder what the body has to do with it. We are accustomed to think of the body, our physical being, as doing only what the mind and the heart tell it to do. But it's not that simple. The body has ingrained habits. I find that, left to itself, my car tends to follow the routes which it has become accustomed to and sometimes has to be forcibly reminded to go where I want it to go. That's because there are times when I'm on autopilot and the body takes over. The body has habits, desires, appetites, and addictions which we have reinforced and magnified by what we have led it into and taught it. In particular, we have taught our brains (the brain is, of course, part of the body) some deep-rooted habits and patterns of response and thinking, which through repetition come to have a physical basis. These ingrained habits (at least the sinful ones, because there are good ones too) have to be dealt with as part of the long project of Christian character formation. The neuroplasticity of the brain, which enables it to go on reorganizing itself throughout life, makes it possible to disempower bad habits and gradually establish new and better ones.

Paul understood the problem:

> Wretched man that I am! Who will deliver me from this body of death?
>
> *Romans 7:24*

He also knew the answer:

> . . . if you live according to the flesh you will die, but if by the Spirit you put to death the deeds of the body, you will live.
>
> *Romans 8:13*

The phrase about putting to death the deeds of the body by the Spirit brings us back to the arena of divine-human cooperation, always understood as being ultimately a work of God's grace. Paul urges the Galatians to "sow to the Spirit"[66] and tells the Colossians to "put to death" the wrong set of habits and "put on" the right one.[67] We are to adopt the practices which cumulatively will put the deeds of the body to death, and as we do so, we will find the Spirit coming alongside to enable and assist us.

Spiritual disciplines

What are these practices? They are the spiritual disciplines. There is no exhaustive list of spiritual disciplines because the Holy Spirit is well able to lead individuals into practices which will answer to their needs and circumstances. But these are some of the things involved: worship, sacraments, reading scripture, fasting, prayer, meditation, solitude, silence, confession, thanksgiving . . .

We see Jesus teaching the use of spiritual disciplines when he tells the disciples that their giving, prayer, and fasting should all be done "in secret" if they want to receive a reward from the Father who sees "in secret".[68] He is telling them how to deal with the ingrained human lust for the praise of other people: kill it off by doing all those things in secret. We cannot by direct effort get rid of the desire for human praise, but there is something we can do which in the long run will starve that desire and do it to death: do the things we seek praise for in secret, so that nobody can see what we're up to and nobody can praise us.

Direct effort will often be useless in dealing with our sinful habits, but spiritual disciplines enable us to put in place practices which will give space to the Holy Spirit to do what we cannot by our own effort achieve. Spiritual disciplines work mostly by *indirection*. An athlete trains for their chosen sport by doing a lot of other things besides just the sport itself: sprinters don't spend all their time sprinting—other disciplines such as weight training will be vital. This, again, is the method of indirection: seeking success not always by tackling the issue head-on but by engaging in practices which will indirectly build the capacity to attain the central goal.

Pray for one another

Personal spiritual disciplines are important, but they are not the whole story in the development of Christian character. There will be times for all of us when we need the help of our brothers and sisters, particularly in the confession of sin. James tells his readers:

> . . . confess your sins to one another and pray for one another,
> that you may be healed.
>
> *James 5:16*

I think there is a good case for taking James' instruction to apply to more than just physical healing. Our souls need healing too. We carry with us weaknesses and wounds from the past which need to be dealt with if we are to find true freedom in Christ.

These wounds are essentially of two kinds: the kind where we are at fault and need to receive God's forgiveness, and the kind where somebody else is at fault and we may need to extend forgiveness to them.

The hurts done to us may range from someone's thoughtless but hurtful comment all the way to physical violence, sexual abuse, rape, or the murder of a loved one. Any sin against us, even if seemingly trivial to the casual observer or even the perpetrator, can leave a mark in our souls which hinders the renewed heart from living out the fullness of life promised by Jesus. We may need help from a trusted fellow Christian to work through these things. Having a spiritual director or soul friend is one way of meeting that need. Another is what is variously called "inner healing" or "the healing of memories". Some Christians belong to a small confidential cell group which provides a safe context for this kind of prayer.

Confession of sin sometimes needs to go beyond what we are personally responsible for. Daniel confessed the sins of his forebears.[69] There may be times when we become aware of the sins of previous generations in our family, and we need to confess their sins in order to free ourselves and subsequent generations from the results of their bad choices. It's a kind of spiritual gene therapy.

Character and community

Christian character is formed in community—above all, the community of the church. Many of the spiritual disciplines are meant to be practised in community. There are dimensions of prayer and mutual encouragement which can only take place in community. The church is designed to be a loving, supportive, forgiving, patient, challenging, truth-telling community whose members will spur one another on to grow in likeness to Jesus Christ.

Some reflections

My reflections on this chapter are thoughts about how church culture needs to change—what we need to do to ensure holiness is restored to its rightful place amongst us.

1. Embracing suffering

We need to be clear about the place of suffering in the Christian life. One of the saddest experiences for a Christian pastor is to see someone come to faith, grow in the things of the Spirit with enthusiasm and commitment, and then, when something painful happens to them or those they love, give up—often in outraged surprise that God, who is supposed to love them, has allowed whatever it is to befall them. At one level this is something we should expect—Jesus predicted in the Parable of the Sower that some would give up under pressure. But if we taught Christians from the beginning that suffering was part of the deal and had a key role to play in the development of their character, that might make a significant difference to the dropout rate. If all Christians were able to encourage those who are suffering that God would work for good for them in their suffering, we would all gain. We're not talking about a glib dismissal of people's pain; we will need all the more to weep with those who weep. But suffering is here to stay this side of the new creation, so we would do well to come to terms with it, and even, according to Paul and James, rejoice in it.

2. Confronting failure

We need to create a church culture where moral failure is neither condemned nor covered up. We are not good at knowing what to do with our own character defects and moral failures, or those of our fellow Christians. Instead of recognizing that such things are there to be confronted with confidence that the Holy Spirit will help us, we either panic and give up in despair, or we shrug our shoulders and decide that it's no good expecting anything better. The good news of the New Testament's emphasis on the development of character is that there is a way forward. Believing and teaching this could change the culture of our churches, such that messing up would not lead to shame, defensiveness, and the attempt to cover up where we've gone wrong; instead, we could hope to shape a mutually supportive environment where we knew how to encourage each other in the ways of spiritual discipline and growth. The fact that holiness is not instantaneous and that there is a long process of gradual transformation involved in being disciples of Jesus is good news: it acknowledges that our fragmentary moral progress is not a sign of failure, but the way things work.

3. Normalizing spiritual disciplines

We need to create a culture where the practice of spiritual disciplines is normal—routinely taught and practised. Sometimes we give the impression that these things are for Lent and for the specially keen and committed, and thus we obscure the vital fact that they are part of the bread and butter of being a disciple. We fail to make it plain that they have a very specific purpose: to create space for the Holy Spirit to land in our lives and do God's work.

4. Beginning with the end in mind

Finally, "beginning with the end in mind" should supply the motivation to take seriously the call to grow in likeness to Jesus. Knowing that a well-formed character is a preparation for sharing in the rule of God's new creation makes a very big difference to the attitude we take to our own and others' needs to change. As things stand, we are often reduced to trying to keep to the rules we find in scripture and telling others to do the same. To put it crudely, there doesn't seem to be much point or pay-off in putting serious effort into change. If we're going to heaven anyway (and there's not much to do there), why bother? Rule-keeping doesn't feel good at the best of times (it's hardly the fullness of life promised by Jesus), and it's particularly hard to commend in a culture like ours which dislikes rules anyway. There *are* rules, to be sure. There *are* things which please God and things which displease him. The New Testament repeatedly urges us to find out what pleases him and act accordingly. But rules can only *support* right conduct by showing us where we are going wrong; rules in themselves have no power to *enable* right conduct.

Anybody who has taken young children tenpin bowling will know that they (and some adults as well) will probably need the help of barriers to prevent the ball from falling into the troughs either side of the bowling alley, and thus failing to score. The barriers are not put in place for those who are any good at bowling. They don't need them. They have developed the ability to send the ball straight down the track and hit the pins. Beginners haven't learned that yet and need the help of the barriers. Most people want to get beyond needing the barriers to having enough skill to send the ball straight down the track. They want it, and they can see that it's possible because the people in the next alley are not using the barriers. Thus the beginners have hope that something better and more exciting really is possible. So it is with disciples of Jesus. We need to know what the rules are, but if that's all we're given then we're likely to give up any serious attempt to change and grow.

C. S. Lewis gives imaginative expression to the purpose of Christian character formation in fitting us for glory, referring—as I did earlier in this chapter—to Jesus' parable of the dishonest manager in Luke 16:

> There is in our present pilgrim condition plenty of room (more room than most of us like) for abstinence and renunciation and mortifying our natural desires. But behind all asceticism the thought should be, "Who will trust us with the true wealth if we cannot be trusted even with the wealth that perishes?" Who will trust me with a spiritual body if I cannot control even an earthly body? These small and perishable bodies we now have were given to us as ponies are given to schoolboys. We must learn to manage: not that we may some day be free of horses altogether but that some day we may ride bare-back, confident and rejoicing, those greater mounts, those winged, shining and world-shaking horses which perhaps even now expect us with impatience, pawing and

snorting in the King's stables. Not that the gallop would be of any value unless it were a gallop with the King; but how else—since He has retained His own charger—should we accompany Him?[70]

CHAPTER 6

Charism

In the previous chapter we touched on some aspects of the work of the Spirit in shaping Christian character—enabling disciples to *be* more like Jesus. I now want to explore the gifts of the Spirit in enabling disciples to *do* the things that Jesus did.

The Holy Spirit and the Kingdom of God

The arrival of the Kingdom of God precipitates an outpouring of the Spirit of God. In the early chapters of Luke's Gospel there is a flurry of activity by the Spirit:

1. The angel tells Zechariah that the son who will be born to him will be filled with the Holy Spirit from his mother's womb.
2. Gabriel tells Mary that the Holy Spirit will come upon her to conceive the Messiah.
3. Elizabeth is filled with the Holy Spirit when Mary comes to visit her.
4. After the birth of his son John, Zechariah is filled with the Spirit and prophesies.
5. The elderly Simeon has multiple Holy Spirit experiences:
   a. the Spirit is *upon* him,

   b. the Spirit *reveals* to him that he will see the Messiah before he dies,

   c. he comes into the Temple *in* the Spirit and prophesies over Jesus.

Luke is telling us that a new era is dawning. Gabriel tells Mary what will be different about this new dawn:

> . . . nothing *will be* impossible with God.
>
> *Luke 1:3 (my italics)*

The tense is future, something quite often missed in the English translations, which make Gabriel say that all things *are* possible with God (which is true but hardly a new idea). Gabriel's message is much more significant than that. He is telling Mary that those caught up in the Jesus event will experience the power of God released in ways hitherto confined to exceptional people in exceptional times. This is the Kingdom which Jesus will inaugurate and over which Jesus will preside.

The fact that it is Gabriel who brings this message is in itself significant. He it was who gave Daniel a vision "for the time of the end"[71] and responded to Daniel's prayer of repentance for Israel's sins with the message that:

> Seventy weeks are decreed about your people and your holy city, to finish the transgression, to put an end to sin, and to atone for iniquity, to bring in everlasting righteousness, to seal both vision and prophet, and to anoint a most holy place.
>
> *Daniel 9:24*

The arrival of Gabriel (who makes no other appearance in scripture apart from these episodes in Luke) is a hint that what he prophesied to Daniel centuries previously is now going to be fulfilled. The long-awaited resolution of Israel's difficult history and the fulfilment of her long-delayed hopes are about to take place, and the work of the Holy Spirit is central.

Are spiritual gifts for today?

The Holy Spirit is clearly at work in the ministry of Jesus. The gifts of the Spirit are also clearly in evidence in the book of Acts, in the writings of Paul, and in the other New Testament documents. But are they meant for the church today as well? That is disputed. While all Christians believe in the Holy Spirit, not all Christians believe that the gifts of the Spirit are for today. Some believe that these gifts were for the apostolic age only and were meant to cease once the work of the apostles was complete; if that is true, then seeking these gifts can only lead to deception and potentially dangerous aberrations. Alongside this theological doubt, there is often also an anxiety about how these gifts will function in practice— they can seem messy, unpredictable, and frankly weird at times, an impression which is backed up by the sometimes flaky behaviour of some charismatics.

The theological question

Let's consider first the theological objection. This is based primarily on the passage in 1 Corinthians 13 where Paul says that the gifts of tongues, prophecy, and knowledge will cease "when the perfect comes".[72]

The question is: what does Paul mean by "the perfect"? The usual view from those who believe spiritual gifts are finished is that "the perfect" refers to the completion of the canon of scripture: once you've got the whole Bible, you don't need any other means of knowing and hearing God.

Is that what Paul means? The perfection to which he refers is further amplified as "seeing face to face" and "knowing fully, even as I have been fully known". The apostle can only be talking about meeting *God* face to face and knowing *God* fully as God already knows him fully, a state of affairs which can only come about either at death or at the renewal of all things in the new creation. That kind of unmediated personal encounter and unalloyed mutual personal knowledge is not available otherwise, not even through scripture. That will only come when the End comes, for only the End answers to his definition of what is "perfect". Paul is saying in very clear terms that spiritual gifts will last until the end of this age, at which point, being partial and fragmentary, they will no longer be needed.

Spiritual gifts and the authority of scripture

The theological objection to the continuing practice of spiritual gifts is fundamentally a concern that the supreme authority of scripture should not be compromised. The concern is not groundless. It is unfortunately true that unstable and badly instructed Christians can be led astray in this way. It is also true that leaders can lead others astray through the abuse of spiritual gifts. But the fact that spiritual gifts can be abused is not a reason for abolishing their right and proper use. Rightly used, the gifts are no threat to the authority of scripture.

The point can be illustrated from the Old Testament. There is an intriguing incident which foreshadows this anxiety that prophecy might undermine the authority of scripture. In the book of Numbers, Moses gathers seventy of the elders of Israel, and the Lord takes some of the Spirit that is upon him and gives it to them. As a result they prophesy. Two of the elders are not present at this gathering but they still prophesy. This looks to Joshua like something out of order so he urges Moses to put a stop to it:

> But Moses said to him, "Are you jealous for my sake? Would that all the Lord's people were prophets, that the Lord would put his Spirit on them!"
>
> ***Numbers 11:29***

Moses is the one through whom the authoritative word of God comes to his people. He is the mediator of the covenant and the one who brings the Law to Israel. And yet he is not at all worried that the word of God through him is in danger from prophecy. Far from it: he longs that all should prophesy, not just the elders.

In the new covenant, Moses' longing is fulfilled: the gift of prophecy is open to all, and rightly handled, it is no threat to the authority of scripture.

In Romans 12 Paul gives instruction as to how spiritual gifts should be exercised, including the gift of prophecy:

> Having gifts that differ according to the grace given to us, let us use them: if prophecy, in proportion to our faith;
>
> **Romans 12:6**

This is how most English versions translate Paul's words, but there are some which render the word translated "proportion" as "agreement" or "right relationship" or "pattern". Thus the second part of the verse would read like this:

> . . . if prophecy, in agreement with the faith;
>
> **(my translation)**

This is the meaning suggested by what is usually regarded as the premier Lexicon of New Testament Greek.[73] It seems to me very likely that Paul is not limiting the exercise of prophecy according to the faith of the individual. Rather, he is giving explicit instruction that prophecy must never depart from, or contradict, the content of apostolic faith.

The purpose and operation of the gifts

The gifts are given to release the love and power of God into people's lives. In the last resort the proof of the pudding is in the eating: the authenticity or otherwise of spiritual gifts must be judged by their fruit. So having explored gifts of healing in Chapter 4, I propose now to look at the spiritual gifts of tongues and prophecy, and leave the reader to judge their value.

The gift of tongues

First, tongues. This is a gift which some people are embarrassed should be included in the canon of scripture. The word is weird and the experience sounds as if it must be weird too. But there is no need to be embarrassed—either by the word or the experience. The word means simply "languages" and is probably translated "tongues" both because we have inherited the archaic wording of the Authorized Version and to distinguish this as a spiritual gift rather than something learned in the normal way. There is nothing weird about the experience of speaking in tongues; there is no question of being out of control or "ecstatic", despite the *New English Bible*'s translation of tongues in 1 Corinthians 12 as "the gift of ecstatic utterance". Speaking in tongues is like speaking any other language: you start and stop at will and you are entirely in control of the speed and volume of what you're saying.

Paul speaks of both human and angelic tongues, so we should expect that—at least sometimes—identifiable human languages are being spoken, as in Acts 2 on the Day of Pentecost. There are many well-documented instances of this. Some years ago I was a member of a team speaking at a conference in Scandinavia for overseas missionaries. During worship one afternoon there was a time of singing in tongues. Afterwards, one of the missionaries, who was serving in East Africa, approached one of the team members and asked: "Do you speak Swahili?"

"No", the team member replied. "Why do you ask?"

"Because just now you were singing to Jesus in Swahili."

I don't know what the long-term value of that experience was to the overseas missionary, but to the team it was a small reminder that in worship heaven touches earth, and that God can sometimes surprise us by working in us things which are quite beyond our unaided human capacity.

I suspect (though I cannot prove) that the experience of speaking, and being heard to speak, in a known but unlearned language happens a good deal on the frontiers of the church: in pioneer mission situations and where the church is undergoing persecution.

For most of us, most of the time, the primary purpose of tongues is our own personal edification:

> The one who speaks in a tongue builds up himself . . .
>
> *1 Corinthians 14:4*

Speaking in tongues is entirely under the speaker's control but it bypasses the conscious mind. You don't know what you're talking about, which is both a weakness and a strength. The weakness, as Paul is at pains to explain in 1 Corinthians, is that most of the time tongues don't do anybody but the speaker any good. The strength, on the other hand, is precisely in bypassing the mind. What is happening is direct spirit-to-spirit communication: the Holy Spirit communicating with our spirit. Alternatively, one could describe it as "heart-to-heart": the new heart which is the gift of God in the new covenant being enabled to receive strength from the heart of God. It is one of the ways in which the Kingdom comes to us; like all the spiritual gifts, it is heaven connecting with earth.

Practising the gift of tongues is another kind of spiritual discipline to add to those mentioned in Chapter 5. It does you good. Often I pray in tongues while driving (on my own) and I find—I hope this doesn't sound trivial—that it makes me a better driver: more careful and more alert. More significantly, Jackie Pullinger, who recently completed fifty years of working with the poor in Hong Kong and across South East Asia, found a new effectiveness in ministry through speaking in tongues for fifteen minutes every day by the clock.[74] To this day, because of her teaching and training, people are coming off heroin painlessly through using the gift of tongues.

Releasing the gift

Paul wanted everyone to speak in tongues,[75] by which he appears to mean that he wants everybody to use this gift in private, because it's not for everybody to exercise in public.[76] For this reason, I believe the gift is available to all Christians, as was the case on the Day of Pentecost. It's not compulsory but it's there to be used if you want to. It's helpful to think of it as a gift to be *released in us* rather than *received by us*. It's there as latent potential already—you just have to ask for its release and then start speaking, but not in your own language. Like anything new, it may be fragmentary and hesitant at first, but fluency comes with perseverance. And it's quite likely that you will think you are making it up. Like everything else in the Christian life, it's by faith. Trust God and keep going, and you will in the long run know it's for real.

The gift of prophecy

Wayne Grudem has a useful definition of New Testament prophecy as "speaking merely human words to report something God brings to mind".[77]

This definition is helpful because:

1. It emphasizes that the one giving a prophecy is not speaking words of direct divine authority which might give rise to some confusion or competition with the words of scripture: prophecy needs to be tested and can be challenged and corrected.
2. It gives a good idea of what prophecy mostly feels like in practice. Prophecy comes in different forms: as an impression, a form of words, a mental picture, a Bible reference, even a physical sensation. The one giving the prophecy has to communicate what comes to him or her as best they can.
3. It goes some way to demystifying the experience. Like most spiritual gifts, most of the time it is quite an ordinary business.

Of course, there will be times when there is a heightened sense of the presence of God and a super-charged atmosphere. But those things are not necessary or even especially common. Prophecy is one of the ways the Kingdom comes, enabling heaven and earth to connect as they were meant to. This is what we were created for; it is our natural condition and therefore does not need to be hyped up.

4. It indicates that prophecy is not primarily about predicting the future.

Paul sets out the purpose of New Testament prophecy as follows:

> . . . the one who prophesies speaks to people for their upbuilding and encouragement and consolation.
>
> *1 Corinthians 14:3*

Prophecy is never meant to be condemning, but always a channel for the love and grace of God to flow through.

Here, by way of illustration and to put some flesh on these bare bones, are two instances of the gift of prophecy in action (one very ordinary and another a bit more out of the ordinary).

Prophecy in action

At the same conference in Scandinavia already referred to, the team did their best to give prophetic words to the missionaries for their encouragement. On one occasion I remember looking at the wife of one couple. I knew nothing about her or her husband and had not spoken to them before, but I had a sense, which I hoped was from the Holy Spirit, that the wife was very concerned about what provision there would be for her small child when they went to the mission field. I also sensed that God wanted to reassure her that he knew and cared about her concern. So, rather tentatively, I went up to her during a coffee break and told

her what I sensed the Holy Spirit wanted to say to her. As I spoke, her
eyes filled with tears and she acknowledged that yes, this was true, they
were bound for South Africa (I think it was a remote area), and she was
so grateful to hear that God knew and cared about her anxiety. At one
level, this could seem trivial—so small a thing as to be hardly worth
mentioning. But for this young woman it meant at least two things. In the
first place, it allayed some of her fears and helped her to trust God more.
In the second place (and this is probably the more significant in the long
run), it strengthened her awareness of God's love for her. We know that
God knows everything—in theory. In theory, she knew that God knew
about her anxiety for her child. But hearing it from a third party, who
had no natural way of knowing this, was for her a token of the personal,
loving, practical concern of God. The whole experience was a (small but
real) communication of grace.

My second example comes from Adolf Hitler's god-daughter (I said it
was more out of the ordinary). Rosemarie Claussen's father was a German
police general during the 1930s in Hamburg and Berlin. Shortly after
Rosemarie was born, her father was responsible for overseeing a visit
to Hamburg by the Führer and therefore came into personal contact
with the man himself. Discovering how thrilled the general was over the
birth of his daughter, Hitler took it into his head that he should be the
child's godfather, which is one of those offers you can't refuse. During the
Olympics the general became Hitler's personal bodyguard. However, the
general was a committed Christian who secretly enabled Jews to escape
Nazi persecution. When the Gestapo discovered this, the general was
offered the choice of committing suicide (in which case his death would
be attributed to natural causes and he would receive a funeral with full
military honours) or seeing his whole family deported. The general chose
suicide. When the war came there began a time of intense suffering for
Rosemarie and her family which was even worse when the war ended. She
spent years in terror of Russian troops and the horrific atrocities which
she saw. However, she survived, got married, and found healing for her
painful memories through Christian faith. In due course, she and her
husband became involved in Christian ministry, speaking widely about
the power of forgiveness.

After the collapse of Soviet communism, Rosemarie and her husband were invited to visit a prison in one of the Baltic states. Most of the prisoners were Russians. Rosemarie began to speak about forgiveness, and as she spoke her attention was drawn to a young man in the front row who was sobbing uncontrollably. Then she began to sense that the Holy Spirit was telling her to go and put her arms round this young man's shoulders. She protested inwardly that he was dirty and smelly. But the inner urging persisted, so she prayed again, asking this time if she was supposed to hug all the Russians. No, she sensed it was just this one. So she went over to him and put her arm round his shoulders, whereupon he burst into tears again. After the service he told her his story. He had been brought up in a Pentecostal church where his father was the pastor, the kind of pastor who refused to compromise with the regime's demands. The son had turned against God under the influence of Soviet teaching on atheism and had betrayed his father to the KGB, who came to the house to take his father away. As the father left the house he said to his son:

> I forgive you and as a sign of it, one day, someone from far away
> will come and put his arms around your shoulder.[78]

That was the last time he saw his father. When Rosemarie put her arms round his shoulder, he knew that his father had forgiven him. The prophecy had been fulfilled. And the young man went on to become a pastor in that prison.

My first example illustrates the ordinary nature of much New Testament prophecy. It's the kind of thing which happens a lot in church communities which practise spiritual gifts, and the kind of thing which the sceptic could easily rubbish, but which means a lot to those personally involved.

My second example is harder to dismiss unless you have a very strong commitment to scepticism. It's the kind of thing only God could do: who else can orchestrate such a coming-together of people to fulfil a prophecy which only one of them knew about? You either have to believe it or write it off as a pious fiction. And it beautifully illustrates several things: the grace of God in reaching out to this young man and turning his life round, the providence of God in redeeming Rosemarie's years of pain by enabling her to speak from experience about the importance of forgiveness, and the power of a disciple's risky obedience in doing what the Holy Spirit told her to do.

Prophecy and the word of knowledge

So much by way of defence of the reality and relevance of spiritual gifts for today. I want now briefly to address what seems to me a widespread confusion in the understanding of the gift of prophecy. I have in mind the way Pentecostals and charismatics usually talk about the spiritual gift which Paul calls "the word of knowledge". A common definition of the word of knowledge is:

> ... the ability of one person to know what God is currently doing or intends to do in the life of another person. It can also be defined as knowing the secrets of another person's heart.[79]

The problem with this definition is that it looks remarkably close to the way *prophecy* and the ministry of *prophets* are described in the New Testament. For example:

1. When Jesus tells the Samaritan woman that she has had five husbands and is currently living with someone who is not her husband, her immediate response is: "Sir, I perceive that you are a prophet."[80]

2. When Jesus is anointed by a sinful woman in the house of a Pharisee, the Pharisee says to himself: "If this man were a prophet, he would have known who and what sort of woman this is who is touching him, for she is a sinner."[81] Jesus then demonstrates conclusively that he is a prophet according to the Pharisee's definition by revealing that he knows exactly the secrets of the Pharisee's heart.

3. Paul describes the ideal operation of the gift of prophecy as follows: " . . . if all prophesy, and an unbeliever or outsider enters, he is convicted by all, he is called to account by all, the secrets of his heart are disclosed, and so, falling on his face, he will worship God and declare that God is really among you."[82]

It is prophecy, not the word of knowledge, which reveals the secrets of people's hearts—so that God can get through to them and bless them. That is why Paul makes such a big thing of prophecy, whereas he says very little about the word of knowledge. A friend of mine once remarked that it was curious that there had been such a revival of the word of knowledge alongside prophecy in recent times when it is prophecy which Paul especially commends. I have come to believe that it is more than curious: it is a mistake.

Does it matter? Not hugely perhaps, but, as always when we misidentify what scripture is talking about, it means we are missing out on something. Wayne Grudem offers a definition of the word of knowledge: "the ability to speak in a way that gives true knowledge to people—especially knowledge of Scripture and knowledge of God".[83]

This is what we get in the best scholarship, in the best preaching and teaching, and in the words of any Christian who is gifted by God to give insight into the truth of scripture and the ways of God. We need that kind of insight and it would be good to recognize that it is a spiritual gift. Among other things, this would help us to understand that spiritual gifts don't have to be spooky or feel "supernatural" to be real.

Gifts and ministries

Spiritual gifts *(charismata)* are gifts of grace *(charis)*. One writer called them "gracelets". They are primarily events rather than endowments. This is particularly clear in the case of healing, since Paul speaks of "gifts of healings",[84] but it applies also to prophecy. The gifts are *things which happen*—ways in which the Kingdom comes—when Christians expect them (and sometimes when they don't). (The exception is the gift of tongues, which is an endowment which can be summoned up at will.) I think it's better to speak of exercising *a* gift of healing rather than seeking to receive *the* gift of healing. Those who habitually and effectively operate in particular gifts may, over the course of time, be recognized as having a ministry in that area. But that doesn't mean that the rest of us can't exercise any gift when the need arises.

Some reflections

Finally, some reflections on the importance of spiritual gifts.

1. Why we need spiritual gifts

Are spiritual gifts important? Or is it that they were once important but are now well past their sell-by date? Or are they just a fad, an irrelevant sideshow which distracts from the main event? It will be obvious by now that I believe they are an essential part of the equipment of the church in every age.

We are called by Jesus to imitate him, to be his followers, which—among other things—involves doing the kind of things which he did. For instance:

1. Jesus lived a life of constant communion with his Father. So Paul exhorts the Thessalonians to "pray without ceasing".[85] The gift of tongues is one of the ways—only one, but still one—in which we can learn to do that.
2. Jesus frequently healed the sick. The gifts of healings described by Paul enable us—falteringly but still genuinely—to imitate Jesus.
3. Jesus frequently spoke pointedly into people's lives, revealing the secrets of their hearts in such a way as to open them up to the love

and grace of God. The gift of prophecy so warmly commended by Paul enables us to learn to follow suit.

The church has often, in practice, restricted the meaning of discipleship to living out the Sermon on the Mount. For many people much of the time, following Jesus has been understood as following his moral teaching. Nobody wants to deny that or downplay it. But there is much more involved if we are to be anywhere near faithful to the wider perspective of the New Testament.

The corollary of restricting the meaning of discipleship to living out the Sermon on the Mount has sometimes been that spiritual gifts are cordoned off to be the province of special people—saints, religious, hermits etc. If you want a word or a touch from God you seek out a holy person. Or you go to a holy *place*—Lourdes, Czestochowa, or any of the many other pilgrimage sites. The New Testament picture is much more democratic than this. It holds out a vision where everybody who believes in Jesus is able to have a go at doing the things that Jesus did.

2. Why we are wary of spiritual gifts

What's not to like? Why are so many in the church dismissive, sceptical, or downright hostile to the use of spiritual gifts? I have explored briefly some of the theological objections and suggested that they don't add up to a real case against. I think there are other motives in play besides the strictly theological concerns.

Spiritual gifts are partial and fragmentary, as Paul makes clear. It is quite possible to get things wrong. Does that matter? Only if we pretend to get everything right and lay claim to some kind of infallibility. If we go around saying, "Thus says the Lord . . .", we put undue pressure on people to accept what we say, we make it much harder to evaluate the gift, and we run the risk of ending up with a lot of egg on our faces when it becomes clear that the Lord has not said what we attributed to him. These issues can be dealt with by means of proper teaching and appropriate oversight of the exercise of gifts.

Spiritual gifts can be messy—in a good way. Spiritual gifts are meant to get to the heart of people and their problems, and people's lives are often messy. The difficulty we have is that church is supposed by many people to be free of mess. We are supposed to behave with perfect decorum, to live lives of smiling contentment and effortless niceness. Sometimes the church's liturgy is used to maintain this façade, ruling out nearly all spontaneity. I believe liturgy is a great gift and the church is poorer without it, but liturgy at its best is meant to enable spontaneity, not to suppress it; to create the framework within which the Holy Spirit can do his work, rather than protect us from it.

The book of Proverbs has this to say:

> Where there are no oxen, the manger is clean,
> but abundant crops come by the strength of the ox.
>
> *Proverbs 14:4*

It's easy for churches to be much more bothered about keeping the manger clean than about bringing in the harvest. Derek Kidner's Commentary describes this proverb as a plea for "the readiness to accept upheaval, and a mess to clear up, as the price of growth".[86]

Upheaval and clearing up mess place demands on churches and their leadership which not all are willing to accept. But these things are part of the cost of discipleship, of seeing the Kingdom come, of facilitating the progress of the gospel.

3. How we handle spiritual gifts

I mentioned earlier in the chapter that the gifts are manifestations of grace. This leads to an important warning. The fact that somebody manifests a spiritual gift says nothing about their holiness or spiritual maturity. The New Testament church which was most eager for spiritual gifts was also probably the most confused and chaotic in lifestyle, as Paul's first letter to Corinth bears witness. Some very dodgy people can sometimes demonstrate amazing spiritual power: look at the story of Samson in the Old Testament. Leaders must beware of being over-impressed by people with amazing spiritual gifts. They may be amazing Christians (in which case they will use the gifts with love and humility) but they may just be experiencing amazing grace. It is vital not to be controlled by the spiritually gifted but spiritually immature, or to let them control the church.

It is also vital not to draw the opposite conclusion and decide that spiritual gifts are only for the immature and are best avoided because of the hassle they cause. Paul praised the Corinthians for their concern for spiritual gifts and sought to channel their enthusiasm—he never suggested they should give them up or tried to damp down their desire for them. Spiritual gifts are here to stay—until the Kingdom comes in fullness.

CHAPTER 7

Christology

We have begun to explore Jesus' call to his disciples to imitate not only his life but his work, not only his attitudes but his actions—to do the things that he did, including the things that we label supernatural. There are no doubt many questions that one might want to raise when faced with the call and commission of Jesus, but one of the most common and urgent is this: Jesus was the incarnate Son of God—a man, certainly, but so much more than a man; God himself walking this earth. How, then, can mere humans be expected to do what he did? Surely he had an impossibly unfair advantage, and he is simply asking too much of us?

It is a fair question. Unless there is a satisfactory answer which works both at the level of theological truth and pastoral practice, then we can't make progress.

Jesus' relationship to the Father

I believe we find Jesus' own answer to this question in John Chapter 5. Here he heals a man at the pool of Bethesda in Jerusalem on the Sabbath. The authorities are enraged, firstly that he does "work" on the Sabbath, and secondly that in response he justifies his action by saying that he is continuing his Father's work, thus "making himself equal with God". Jesus then goes on to speak at some length about the nature of his relationship with the Father, beginning with these words:

> Truly, truly, I say to you, the Son can do nothing of his own
> accord, but only what he sees the Father doing. For whatever the
> Father does, that the Son does likewise. For the Father loves the
> Son and shows him all that he himself is doing. And greater works
> than these will he show him, so that you may marvel.
>
> *John 5:19–20*

The first thing to note is that Jesus does not seek to refute the charge of making himself equal with God. He is happy to let that stand. And nothing that he says subsequently is meant to cast any doubt on that basic truth.

What it means to be the Son

The second thing to note is that he chooses to focus on his status as "the Son". John's Gospel applies many titles to Jesus: the Word, the Son of God, the Son of Man, Messiah/Christ. In John 5:19–26 he speaks of himself eight times as simply "the Son", a title he uses of himself only five times in the whole of the rest of this Gospel. And he prefaces what he says with the phrase "Truly, truly", which always indicates that this is a solemn pronouncement requiring serious attention. The clear implication is that he is revealing something very important about the nature of his relationship with the Father—what it means for him to be the Son.

The revelation is simply this: to be the Son is to be entirely dependent on the Father. The Son does nothing of his own accord but only what he sees the Father doing. The life of the Son is a life of communion with the Father, a dialogue where the Father is continually showing the Son what he (the Father) wants him (the Son) to do. All this flows from the Father's love for the Son, where the word for "love" is the love between friends. There is a profound friendship between Father and Son, a loving partnership, expressed in the Son's joyful response to the Father's initiative in all things.

The dependence of the Son in John

This dependence of the Son on the initiative of the Father is a significant theme throughout the Gospel of John. Jesus repeatedly states that:

1. His *works* are not his own but come from the Father. (John 5:19–20)
2. His *judgement* is not his own but comes from the Father. (John 5:30)
3. His *teaching and his message* are not his own but come from the Father. (John 7:16–18, 8:28, 12:49, 14:10, 15:15)
4. He has not come on his own *authority* but was sent by the Father. (John 7:28, 8:42)
5. *Laying down his life and taking it up again* are done in response to his Father's command. (John 10:17–18)

John wants us to understand very clearly what the Son is saying about himself. These five areas of his ministry, some of them referred to several times, cover pretty much all he did. Jesus is at great pains to underline in the clearest possible terms his total dependence on the Father. He will not be satisfied unless that message has been fully understood and taken to heart, because it is not a matter of merely theoretical interest. It is essential to the whole project.

A created being?

Some of the heretics of the early centuries of the church interpreted this passage in John 5 to mean that the Son was inferior to the Father, a created being who—though on a higher plane than ordinary humans—was not properly divine. This view was rightly rejected by the church Fathers because it doesn't fit either with the immediate context, which implicitly affirms Jesus' equality with the Father, or with the rest of the New Testament, which in so many ways affirms his divine status.

The limitations of the Incarnation?

Other interpreters[87] have wanted to suggest that Jesus is talking only about his life on earth. They see these words as expressing Jesus' voluntary restriction on his divine capacities during his earthly life, a temporary accommodation to the limitations of the incarnation. Appeal is often made to Paul's statement in Philippians 2:7 that Jesus "emptied himself". Of what did he empty himself? Was it his divine capacities or his divine privileges? Did he lay aside his ability to know all things and do all things, or did he lay aside his privilege of exemption from pain, suffering, misunderstanding, hunger, tiredness, human malice and hatred, and ultimately death itself?

There are several difficulties with the suggestion that Jesus laid aside his divine capacities at the incarnation. In the first place, how would that square with his claim to be the perfect representation of the Father, that he and the Father are one, that whoever has seen him has seen the Father? If Jesus is God minus the divine capacities for knowledge and power, then he is not a full representation of the Father. And secondly, if incarnation necessitates being emptied of these divine capacities, what does that say about the union of humanity and divinity in the person of Jesus which continues forever in heaven after his earthly life? Surely—since he does not divest himself of his humanity at the Ascension—Jesus must lose some of his divinity forever?

It makes much better sense of the whole biblical picture to say that Jesus emptied himself of his divine privilege of immunity from the suffering endemic to a fallen world.

A third way

So far, we have considered two possible interpretations of Jesus' teaching in John 5: either that he is inferior to the Father, a superior kind of creature but not fully divine, or that he is talking about the conditions imposed on him by his incarnate state. There is a third approach to what

Jesus is saying here, which I want to advocate. It is that these verses open a window on the eternal truth about Jesus' relationship with the Father. He is not just talking about his earthly life and the limitations which that imposes. He is talking about the way things are from all eternity. That's why he refers to himself repeatedly and emphatically as "the Son".

Nobody has put this view better than Professor James Packer, who has a good claim to be the foremost Anglican Evangelical theologian of his generation:

> . . . the obedience of the God-man to the Father while He was on earth was not a new relationship occasioned by the incarnation, but the continuation in time of the eternal relationship between the Son and the Father in heaven. As in heaven, so on earth, the Son was utterly dependent upon the Father's will.[88]

The problem we have with this way of understanding what Jesus is saying is that it contradicts the common conception of divinity. This kind of dependence doesn't sit easily with our view of what God is like. We tend to assume that whatever else it may mean to be God, it surely doesn't mean being dependent on anybody or anything. We need to hear the words of Karl Barth, the Swiss Reformed theologian whose *Church Dogmatics* is one of the great monuments of Christian theology:

> . . . we have to see here the other side of the mystery of the *divine nature of Christ* and therefore of *the nature of the one true God*, that he himself is also able and free to render obedience.[89]
>
> *(my italics)*

Barth is saying that the nature of the one true God includes the ability and the freedom to live in dependence, one member of the Trinity offering obedience to another. He is saying that there is more than one way to be God. In fact, there are three ways. The Persons of the Trinity embody in themselves each of those three ways. The way of the Son is to express a complete, profoundly intimate, loving dependence on the Father.

The Nicene Creed

At this point it may help to relate this understanding of the person of the Son to the Creedal statements of the church. Here is the relevant section of the Nicene Creed:

> We believe in one Lord, Jesus Christ,
> the only Son of God,
> eternally begotten of the Father,
> God from God, Light from Light,
> true God from true God,
> begotten, not made,
> of one Being with the Father;
> through him all things were made.

In John 5 Jesus has been accused of claiming equality with God, and nothing is said to diminish or detract from that. As he will explain later in the same Gospel, he is one with the Father and whoever has seen him has seen the Father. The Creed affirms the equality of Father and Son by speaking of their sharing "one being" ("substance" in the older translations). That is, they are composed of the same "stuff", just as a parent and his or her child are composed of the same "stuff".

But there is differentiation between Father and Son. Jesus speaks of a radical, thoroughgoing dependence on his Father in all things. The Creed expresses this in terms of the Son being "eternally begotten" of the Father. The word "begotten" is then repeated and differentiated from "made": "begotten, not made". Begetting is what parents do to acquire children: you beget something, or rather someone, who is made of the same stuff as you are. Humans beget humans. Making is different. You make something which is composed of different stuff. God the Father *begets* God the Son—not in time, as humans do, but "eternally". God *makes* (or creates) the world and humans in it. So by using the term "begotten", the Creed clearly expresses the dependence of the Son on the Father, but makes it equally clear that the Son is not a creature.

C. S. Lewis

C. S. Lewis touches on this question of the dependence of the Son on at least two occasions. Here he is writing to his friend and former pupil, Dom Bede Griffiths:

> About the Son being subject to the Father (as God—of course obviously subject as Man in the Incarnation)—yes, that's what I think: but was contradicted by a theologian. Can you back me up?[90]

The fact that Lewis was contradicted by "a theologian" is not surprising. A lot of theologians have not wanted to go down this route. But equally, the fact that Lewis, who was consistently humble in not overestimating his theological knowledge, wanted his friend to "back him up" says something too. It was not a view he was going to abandon lightly because it had too much in favour of it.

Lewis makes the same point in a different context where he is commenting specifically on John 5:19–20, emphasizing the Creedal orthodoxy of this way of understanding the text:

> The passage does not seem to me to conflict with anything I have learned from the creeds, but greatly to enrich my conception of the Divine sonship.[91]

So if the Creed expresses the dependence of the Son on the Father by using the concept of "begetting", how are we to understand this in relation to John 5:19–20?

St Augustine

The most helpful explanation I have found of what this begetting means in practice comes from St Augustine. Augustine was Bishop of Hippo in North Africa and was one of the greatest theologians the church has ever had.

Fortunately for us, Augustine wrote at length on the Trinity and preached many homilies on John's Gospel, so he deals in some detail with the issues we are exploring, and with John 5:19–20 in particular.

He has a carefully considered way of approaching texts which deal with the relationship of the Father and the Son. In his writing on the Trinity,[92] he puts them into three categories:

1. There are statements about the Father and Son which indicate their unity and equality.
2. There are statements about the Son which relate to his incarnation only and mark him out as less than the Father.
3. There are statements about the Son which "mark him neither as less nor as equal, but only intimate that he is from the Father".

Augustine puts John 5:19 firmly in the third category and summarily dismisses the suggestion that this verse relates to the "creaturely form he took".

In his Homily 20 on John's Gospel[93], Augustine asks what it means to say that the Son is eternally begotten of the Father. If the Son is a Son, he says, then he must have been born. And if he was born, he was born to someone. In order to make it clear that we are not talking about sexual reproduction, Augustine points out that God didn't need to find a mother who would bear his child, "seeing that he uttered the Word from himself": "equal begot equal, eternal begot co-eternal."

The question is: "How . . . does eternal beget eternal?"

Augustine proposes the analogy of a flame and the light which flows from the flame. From the moment the flame is lit, it begins to emit light. The flame does not precede the light it emits: they happen at the same time. So with the eternal begetting of the Son by the Father: "Give me a flame without light, and I will give you God the Father without the Son."

Then he goes on to address the question of what Jesus means when he says that the Son can do nothing on his own, but only what he sees the Father doing. What does this "seeing" consist of? How does it work? His answer is this: ". . . seeing for the Son is the same as being born of the Father."

In the next Homily, 21,[94] he elaborates. He paints the picture which has occurred to several writers on this passage of a son observing his father in his workshop, the father making something so that the son can then copy what his father has made. It's a strictly sequential and separable operation: the father makes, the son observes, the son then copies.

But, says Augustine, this won't do for what we're talking about. If the Father shows the Son what he himself is doing, does that mean that during this time the Son is doing nothing? No, that's not how this works. We know, says Augustine, from the opening verses of John's Gospel that all things were made by the Father through the Son, and "without him nothing was made that has been made."[95] Did the Father make a world and show it to the Son so that he too could have a go at making a world? Of course not. If that were true, says Augustine, "Give us the world, then, which the Son has also made."

Augustine's point is that the works of the Father and the Son are not separable and sequential because the Trinity is inseparable. All the works of the Trinity involve all the Persons of the Trinity at the same time.

Finally, Augustine wraps up his exposition:

> . . . where does the Father show the Son what he is making, if not in the Son himself through whom he does the making?

And again:

> . . . it is not outside of himself that [the Father] shows him something to see, but it is in his very self that he shows him what he is doing.

Relating the Creed to the teaching of Jesus

Augustine brings together the Creedal statements about the Son being
"eternally begotten" of the Father and Jesus' own statement that the Son
can do nothing of his own accord, but only what he sees the Father doing.
He is saying that these two ways of stating the facts describe the same
reality. Being "eternally begotten" means being eternally dependent. It
is a permanent, unchanging relationship. In human experience parents
beget children and then the children grow up, ceasing to be dependent
on their parents, and indeed often finding that in time the relationship
is reversed and the parents become dependent on them. That is not the
way it works with the eternal relationship between the divine Father and
his divine Son. The Son is always in the relationship of dependence. That
is what it means for him to be the Son. When parents beget a child, that
is an event in time which leads on to further events, and the begetting is
left behind. It happened and then things move on. The "begetting" of the
Son by the Father is not a temporal event followed by a different state, a
beginning which leads to something else. It is an eternal reality.

The freedom and dignity of the Son

This kind of dependence is likely to feel, to us, like an affront to the Son's
freedom and dignity. Surely he is constrained and limited by this kind
of relationship to the Father? We are accustomed to view dependence as
a bad thing and to see true freedom and fulfilment as incompatible with
it. Augustine's explanation of the Son seeing what the Father is doing
and doing it himself helps us to see things differently. The dependence
of the Son is not an externally imposed limitation, a restriction on the
freedom of the Son to do his own thing. It is something the Father does
in the Son. Far from being diminishing or disabling, it is empowering.
It is something which wells up inside the Son and flows naturally in him
and through him. The life of the Father and the Son interpenetrate one
another: the Father is in the Son and the Son is in the Father.[96]

Some reflections

The interpretation I am offering of Jesus' words in John 5 is, as I have indicated, controversial. The test of a good hypothesis is that it should not only make sense on its own, but should also illuminate other issues as well. I want to suggest that this way of understanding the teaching of Jesus does just that.

1. The meaning of Sonship

According to John Calvin, the great sixteenth-century Reformer, the early church Fathers viewed John 5:19–20 as teaching something about the relationship between the Father and the Son:

> . . . in these words there is denoted only a distinction of person,
> to make it known that Christ is from the Father . . .

"A distinction of person". In other words, this view shows how Father and Son can be truly differentiated without threatening their equality of substance: there is more than one way to be God. If this is not true, then it is hard to see what the Trinity means. The persons of the Trinity must be distinct.

Calvin's reference to the church Fathers' teaching about the Son being "from the Father" is important. This way of speaking belongs to the classic Christian theological tradition of analysing the relationship between the first and second Persons of the Trinity, as for instance in the quotation given earlier from Augustine's threefold classification of the relevant biblical texts. The fact that the Son is "from the Father" expresses his eternal dependence on the Father. It is equivalent to the statement that he is "eternally begotten" of the Father: this is not a partial or temporary dependence but the most basic fact of his divine life. The Son is "from" the Father as a waterfall is "from" the river which feeds it. The one flows into the other: the waterfall does not exist without the river. To revert to the language of the Creed, one could say that the waterfall is of the same "substance" as the river and equally that it is "begotten" by the river.

2. The incarnation of the Son

The life of whichever member of the Trinity became incarnate would have to be a life of dependence. Human bodily life is dependent life. It comes to us without our consent, it continues on its way with our having only limited control of it (how much can you do about what your internal organs are up to?) and is usually taken from us without our having much say in the matter. Dependence is what Adam and Eve refused in the Garden, and clearing up the mess they initiated was always going to involve doing dependence properly. Apart from an understanding of the eternal dependence of the Son, the way is open to speculate that any member of the Trinity might have taken on human flesh. That is exactly what Thomas Aquinas did,[97] even suggesting that it might have been better if the Father had become incarnate because then the heretic Arius would not credibly have been able to suggest that the Father was inferior to the Son. Apparently, Aquinas withdrew his speculation in the end but it is significant that he thought it worth airing.

3. The person of Christ

I am advocating an understanding of Jesus' divinity in terms of an eternal dependence on the Father. This explains how divinity and humanity could be united in one person in Jesus Christ. Incarnation is only possible if there is a fundamental congruence between humanity and divinity. Otherwise all we have is an oil-and-water mixture which gives us not one person but some kind of hybrid. The Gospels, and subsequent theological reflection, insist that in Jesus Christ we are dealing with one person. Incarnation is only possible if dependence inherently belongs just as much to the Second Person of the Trinity as it does to humanity.

4. The dynamic of discipleship

The dependence of Jesus on the Father points to the inner dynamic of discipleship. Just as Jesus tells us that *he* can do nothing by (or from) himself, so he tells us that *we* can do nothing apart from *him*.[98] When we are incorporated into Christ we are enabled to participate in his doing of the works of the Father. How is this possible? Because we are imitating the Son in his dependence on the Father. He doesn't pull miracles from his back pocket any more than we can. He does what he sees the Father doing. He receives what the Father gives him to do, just as we are called to do. What does this look like? What does it feel like? It is not a spooky or super-spiritual experience necessarily accompanied by goosebumps or supernatural signs. It is not something done *to* us but something God does *in* us by his Spirit. It is a liberating and empowering dynamic. Growing as a disciple involves learning to discern and trust this inner dynamic.

If we are to respond wholeheartedly and confidently to the call of Jesus to be the kind of person that he was and to do the works that he did, then we need to know that this is a reasonable proposition— that *our* obvious inability to deliver in our own strength is matched by *his* total dependence on the Father. Knowing that, like us, Jesus depends on the power of Another gives fresh and deeper meaning to the call to follow him in being Kingdom people and doing Kingdom works.

CHAPTER 8

New Creation

We come now to the issue which has never been far from the surface throughout this book: the question of Christian hope. What future does the gospel of the Kingdom hold out before us? Most Christians today would probably answer in terms of going to heaven when they die. That is a legitimate answer to the question, and one that is fully supported by the witness of the New Testament. Jesus tells the penitent thief:

> Truly, I say to you, today you will be with me in Paradise.
>
> *Luke 23:43*

And as we shall see, Paul reflects in his letter to the Philippians on whether it is time for him to "depart and be with Christ".

The hope of heaven

The hope of heaven is of enormous importance. Other religious or philosophical schemes offer the prospect either of annihilation, or a virtually endless cycle of reincarnations, or being submerged in the ocean of cosmic being, or a long spell in purgatory to fit you for a future with God, or the measuring of your good deeds against your bad to see which comes out on top. Christianity says that if you belong to Christ you will spend eternity with him from the point of death onwards.

At a personal level this is immensely liberating. It answers one of the perennial human questions in a wholly positive way. It offers the security of a guaranteed good future all through life. To those at the extremes of human experience, whether the nearness of one's own death, or the death of a loved one, or the prospect of martyrdom, it is a transforming and life-giving hope.

New heavens and new earth

But the hope of heaven is not the whole story. It answers some important questions at a personal level, but it doesn't answer the bigger questions of the purpose and destiny of God's creation. Nor does it answer the question of the competence of God: did he embark on the project of creation only to abandon it when it went wrong? Is that the best he could do—rescue some faithful adherents and throw everything else in a cosmic dustbin?

During the autumn of 2016 the BBC screened a documentary entitled "Britain's Star Men". The programme shows four astronomers (all of whom have been Professors of Astronomy or Astrophysics at British or American universities) celebrating fifty years of work and friendship by taking a road trip through the southwestern United States to revisit some observatories.

At intervals all four participants have something to say about their religious views. Three of them exhibit various forms of agnosticism, deism, and indifference. The fourth is asked: "Are you afraid of death?" Answer: No, though he's not looking forward to it. He explains: "I'm a Christian. I therefore believe, in principle, in eternal life. But I wonder what you do with eternal life? Eternity is a very long time. There may be telescopes in Heaven. But I don't know what they do with them."

This, as I have suggested, is a truncated version of the Christian hope (and somewhat muddled even about heaven, but that's another story). The tragedy of it should be obvious: here is a man of exceptional intelligence who has succeeded in maintaining his Christian faith in the often hostile environment of academia, and yet his conception of his future is deeply sad. All he can foresee is a very long stretch of time with nothing much to do, and serious doubt about whether what he really cares about will have any place at all. I suspect that he is voicing with unusual candour something not far removed from what many Christians feel when told that heaven is what they have to look forward to.

The hope of heaven is true, but not the whole truth. The whole truth is a much larger vision of "new heavens and a new earth", first mentioned in Isaiah 65 and 66, and picked up and developed in the New Testament. In the final chapters of Revelation we see this vision realized, as heaven comes to earth and the creation is fulfilled at last. When the two parts of God's one creation are renewed and brought together again, a new story begins, from which evil, pain, and suffering are forever excluded. This goes a long way beyond the question of "What will happen to me when I die?" to embrace the whole sweep of God's purpose in launching the project of creation in the first place. When we understand this, we understand that the consistency and competence of God are fully vindicated. He will finish what he started.

Some misunderstandings

There are probably many reasons for the church's failure to maintain the solid hope of new creation at the heart of its teaching. One of these is that there are some New Testament texts which appear to hold out heaven as the principal content of our hope. We need to examine these to clear up any misunderstanding.

Jesus speaks about a great reward in heaven for those who are persecuted because of him,[99] and about laying up treasure in heaven.[100] Since it is this Gospel which contains the most explicit promise of Jesus about the new world that is coming,[101] Matthew can hardly mean us to understand that heaven is the place where these things will be enjoyed; rather, heaven is the place where they are stored up and kept safe.

In the same vein, 1 Peter 1:4 speaks of an inheritance "kept for you in heaven". Again, the point is not that you have to go to heaven to enjoy the inheritance but that heaven is the place of perfect safekeeping. Similarly, Paul speaks in Colossians 1:5 of "the hope laid up for you in heaven". He can hardly mean that heaven is the believer's ultimate destination, because later in the same chapter he speaks of God's purpose "to reconcile to himself all things, whether on earth or in heaven, making peace by the blood of his cross".[102] Heaven and earth are coming together, so there will be no question of going to heaven and leaving earth behind.

Paul reminds the Philippians:

> . . . our citizenship is in heaven, and from it we await a Saviour, the Lord Jesus Christ, who will transform our lowly body to be like his glorious body, by the power that enables him even to subject all things to himself.
>
> *Philippians 3:20-21*

These verses have often been read as a promise that the Philippians will be taken to heaven at the coming of Christ. But this exactly misses the point. Paul is writing to people who belong to a Roman colony, which was Rome's method of spreading Roman culture across the Empire. The Roman citizens in Philippi were not expected to go back to Rome; rather, they were expected to live the Roman life and Roman values where they had been put. The Christian church, says Paul, is expected to live the life of heaven on earth until such time as heaven comes to earth, and everything which resists the life of heaven is finally subdued.

In the same letter, Paul—in prison—toys with the idea that it may be time for him to die:

> For to me to live is Christ, and to die is gain. If I am to live in the flesh, that means fruitful labour for me. Yet which I shall choose I cannot tell. I am hard pressed between the two. My desire is to depart and be with Christ, for that is far better. But to remain in the flesh is more necessary on your account.
>
> *Philippians 1:21-24*

He toys with the idea and rejects it. But later in the same letter he makes clear his willingness to pay any price "that by any means possible I may attain the resurrection from the dead".[103] This time he is unequivocal. There is no question of this being an option he might consider and then reject. Nothing can distract him from the hope of resurrection, of the renewal and restoration of God's creation.

In the following verses he emphasizes his commitment to push on towards that goal: "I press on towards the goal for the prize of the *upward call of God in Christ Jesus.*"[104] The call is not to "heaven", as so many versions mistakenly translate, but to the uphill struggle of doing his part in the battle for the Kingdom.

When the time comes that his own personal end is near, Paul's hope still focuses on the consummation of God's purposes. In prison in Rome he writes:

> . . . I am already being poured out as a drink offering, and the time of my departure has come. I have fought the good fight, I have finished the race, I have kept the faith. Henceforth there is laid up for me the crown of righteousness, which the Lord, the righteous judge, will award to me on that Day, and not only to me but also to all who have loved his appearing.
>
> *2 Timothy 4:6–8*

As he contemplates the closeness of death, his heart is set on the crown of righteousness to be awarded to him "on that Day", which will be a day to be shared with all who have longed for the "appearing" of Jesus. His mind turns not to "heaven" but to the great day when God renews the whole creation at the coming of his Son.

We are not waiting for heaven; rather:

> . . . according to his promise *we are waiting for new heavens and a new earth* in which righteousness dwells.
>
> *2 Peter 3:13 (my italics)*

When Peter and John heal a lame man at the Beautiful Gate of the Temple, a crowd quickly gathers. Peter takes the opportunity to preach the gospel to them:

> Repent therefore, and turn again, that your sins may be blotted out, that times of refreshing may come from the presence of the Lord, and that he may send the Christ appointed for you, Jesus, whom heaven must receive until the time for restoring all the things about which God spoke by the mouth of his holy prophets long ago.
>
> *Acts 3:19–21*

The hope he holds out to them is not heaven, which is where Jesus is for the moment, but "the time for restoring all things".

The achievement of the cross and resurrection

This hope is the achievement of the cross and the resurrection. The resurrection is the visible evidence that death has been defeated through the cross, and victory over death means that sin has been fully and finally dealt with. In the resurrection of Jesus we see bodily life renewed and taken to a fresh dimension of freedom and rich possibility. The risen Jesus is not a ghost or a disembodied spirit; he enjoys a full and joyous bodily existence. The message is clear: all that spoils God's good creation has been, in principle, sorted out. What remains is the full implementation of that victory. And the resurrection not only demonstrates that the victory has been achieved; it also demonstrates what the victory will look like when the new creation comes in fullness.

One of the curious features of the resurrection appearances in the Gospels is that Jesus is sometimes not recognized. It is possible for people to share a long walk and the beginnings of a meal with him not knowing who he is. On other occasions people recognize him immediately. There is both continuity and discontinuity between Jesus as he was before the resurrection and after it. He still has a body which can receive hugs, break bread, eat fish, and build a fire to cook breakfast; but it's a new kind of body which can appear and disappear and to which doors and walls no longer present a barrier. He is the same but different.

Not discarded but transformed

In Paul's long exposition of the meaning of the resurrection in 1 Corinthians 15, this theme of continuity and discontinuity is central:

> Behold! I tell you a mystery. We shall not all sleep, but we shall all be changed, in a moment, in the twinkling of an eye, at the last trumpet. For the trumpet will sound, and the dead will be raised imperishable, and we shall be changed. For this perishable body must put on the imperishable, and this mortal body must put on immortality.
>
> *1 Corinthians 15:51–53*

What is of the earth is not left behind in the resurrection; it is not discarded but transformed.

The same theme of transformation rather than disposal comes to the fore when Paul is talking about the restoration of the non-human creation in Romans 8:

> . . . the creation itself will be set free from its bondage to corruption and obtain the freedom of the glory of the children of God. For we know that the whole creation has been groaning together in the pains of childbirth until now.
>
> *Romans 8:21–22*

The image of childbirth says clearly that in the new creation the old will be fulfilled rather than superseded: it will become more itself rather than less.

This is of enormous importance for our appreciation of Christian hope. One of the results of making heaven the focus of hope is that earthly life is devalued. If our earthly experience is simply to be left behind for us to go to heaven, then it becomes a serious question whether there was much point in having that experience in the first place.

Stephen Kuhrt tells the story of a boy in his church who made a large and impressive Lego castle. Stephen asked if anything went wrong during its construction, to which the boy responded that there had been several times when things went wrong. Stephen then asked him why he hadn't thrown the whole thing away, to which the boy responded with some indignation that his castle was much too valuable just to throw away.[105] God doesn't throw his creation away when it goes wrong. He rescues it and puts it right: he sorts out the problems rather than just throwing in the towel. He doesn't want to send anything or anybody to landfill if he doesn't have to; he is committed to recycling—more than that, to upcycling. His purpose is to rescue us, refurbish us, and fit us for a glorious future.

There is a deep human desire that this life should not simply go to waste. In a recent BBC programme, "Forces of Nature", Professor Brian Cox is shown musing that, given the Einsteinian view of space-time, the lovely things we remember from our past must still be out there somewhere. Maybe so, but there must surely be a corollary to this: if the lovely things from our past are still out there somewhere, so must all the horrible things—the gas chambers and torture chambers, the rapes, the famines, the wars—all the disappointed hopes and all the tragedies of human life. We long for human experience to count for something in the long run rather than simply disappearing into the abyss of time; but if that is to be so, then human experience needs redemption: it has to be purged of all that is harmful and destructive. The cross and resurrection achieve precisely that: the purging *and* the preservation for God's future.

Your labour is not in vain

That is why Paul can end his great chapter on the resurrection with this exhortation not to give up:

> Therefore, my beloved brothers, be steadfast, immovable, always abounding in the work of the Lord, knowing that in the Lord your labour is not in vain.
>
> *1 Corinthians 15:58*

Whatever we do "in the Lord" will last; and the resurrection is the guarantee. Paul has already told these same Corinthians that their "work" will be tested on the Day of Judgement:

> . . . each one's work will become manifest, for the Day will disclose it, because it will be revealed by fire, and the fire will test what sort of work each one has done. If the work that anyone has built on the foundation survives, he will receive a reward. If anyone's work is burned up, he will suffer loss, though he himself will be saved, but only as through fire.
>
> *1 Corinthians 3:13–15*

Some people's work will "survive", will not be burned up; it will live on in some shape in the new creation.

The book of Revelation affirms this truth, that in the Lord our labour is not in vain, and what we do in obedience to God and by the power of his Spirit will last:

> And I heard a voice from heaven saying, "Write this: Blessed are the dead who die in the Lord from now on." "Blessed indeed," says the Spirit, "that they may rest from their labours, for their deeds follow them!"
>
> *Revelation 14:13*

Then I heard what seemed to be the voice of a great multitude,
like the roar of many waters and like the sound of mighty peals
of thunder, crying out,
"Hallelujah!
For the Lord our God
    the Almighty reigns.
Let us rejoice and exult
    and give him the glory,
for the marriage of the Lamb has come,
    and his Bride has made herself ready;
it was granted her to clothe herself
    with fine linen, bright and pure"—
for the fine linen is the righteous deeds of the saints.

Revelation 19:6–8

The more we learn to live the life of heaven in the conditions of earth,
the more of our present lives will be carried over into the new creation.

Living the life of heaven on earth

What does this look like? The whole idea can sound unhelpfully super-spiritual, the kind of behaviour which merits the old jibe about being "so heavenly-minded as to be of no earthly use". The reality, however, is demonstrated in the life of Jesus, who consistently lived the life of heaven in the conditions of earth. He lived the life that is, in the end, the natural condition of humans, where heaven and earth are in full and easy commerce with each other: no gaps in communication, no areas where reception fails. Of all people who have ever lived, Jesus is the last of whom it could be said that he was so heavenly-minded as to be of no earthly use. If you were ill or somebody you loved was ill, if the wine ran out at your wedding, if you were caught in an open boat in a storm, if you were faced with feeding a large crowd with next to nothing in the middle of nowhere, if you'd made a mess of things and needed a fresh start, if your love life had left you a pariah in your own community, if you were wealthy and successful but still searching, if you were dead or somebody you loved was dead . . . in all these things, Jesus was your man.

Well, yes: you might expect that the Son of God would do a good job of bringing heaven to earth. But is there evidence in the New Testament that something not too different is possible for ordinary humans? Yes, of course there is—in many different places. One which is not often remarked on is the account of Paul's shipwreck en route to trial in Rome in Acts 27 and 28.

Paul's shipwreck

Luke spends sixty verses recounting a journey which could have been summarized in six. I suggest that one reason for this, alongside the fact that this was one of the occasions when he himself was present, was that he saw an opportunity for an extended account of Paul in action—a chance to show what life was like with Paul, particularly life with Paul when things were tough.

Several facets of Paul's ability to live the life of heaven in the conditions of earth emerge from these chapters.

First, there is his ability to hear from God in such a way as to give much-needed direction when difficult decisions have to be made. At a critical moment he warns that continuing their journey by ship so late in the year is likely to lead to losing the cargo and to some loss of life. His warning is ignored and they find themselves caught up in a terrible storm. After several days of this, Paul stands up and tells them that he has had a vision of an angel with a message that he will get to Rome because he must stand trial before Caesar, and God has granted him the lives of his companions on the ship.

Second, there is his practicality and shrewdness. Having told the crew that God has granted him their lives, he then says they must run aground on an island. He is nobody's fool: when he sees the sailors trying to escape he tells the centurion and his men that they need to put a stop to this if they want to survive. Then he tells them it's time they ate something, and takes bread and gives thanks to God. The ship runs aground, breaks up, and they eventually land on Malta. The next scene has Paul gathering sticks for a fire. Far from wandering around in some kind of mystical trance, Paul is solidly rooted in the realities of life.

Finally, there is his ability to do the things that Jesus did as a natural part of daily living. A viper comes out of the fire and latches on to Paul's hand. He simply shakes it off back into the fire. No fuss or fanfare, but the locals, having expected that he would swell up and die, decide he must be a god. The company is looked after by the chief man of the island whose father happens to be sick. Paul heals him, which results in the rest of the island's sick coming to the door, and they get healed too.

The whole account reveals Paul as a man in whom heaven and earth meet and are completely at home with each other. Spirituality and practicality, common sense and divine inspiration, spiritual power and down-to-earth getting-on-with-what-needs-to-be-done are perfectly united. But there is no triumphalism—no trace of any suggestion that to live the life of heaven in the conditions of earth entitles anybody to an easy ride. Paul is still on a journey to be put on trial for his life, the ship is still wrecked, everybody on board still has to swim ashore or grab a plank to survive. Suffering is still part of the way that the purpose of God goes forward.

In this age, the followers of Jesus are in a battle for the implementation of his victory on the cross. They are living—to the best of their ability—the life of heaven on earth, which inevitably brings them into conflict with the way the world gets things done. This battle is fought, not with conventional weapons, but with the weapons of Jesus, and that means the battle involves suffering. However, it will not last forever, because Jesus has already won the decisive victory, and this age will, in God's time, give way to the age to come.

What will God's future look like?

What do we know about the promised new creation? What will God's future look like? We know from Revelation 21 that it will be a world where God dwells with humanity, a world from which pain and suffering have been finally removed, a world of great richness and beauty. So much is more or less what people expect of "heaven" in the normal popular understanding. It is good. But it has the feeling of an end more than a beginning, rather like the closing page of a novel where "they all lived happily ever after." As with the novel, all the excitement, all the adventure, and all the anticipation seem to be in the past—over and done with. "Happily ever after" is welcome after the suffering of this present age. What is missing—what the promise of new heavens and new earth supplies—is a fitting consummation to the divine project of creation.

In Revelation 21 the voice of God speaks—for the first time since the opening scene in Chapter 1:

> Behold, I am making all things new.
>
> *Revelation 21:5*

A literal translation would be:

> Behold, new I am making all things.

God is not planning to make *new things* but to make *existing things new*—all of them. He is not discarding his creation. He is renewing everything in that creation. He will remove anything and anybody which is impure, corrupt, sinful, or in any way resistant to his purposes, as the final chapters of Revelation make clear. But all that is good in creation as we know it will be refurbished and refitted for the future purposes of God. Just as God took the broken body of Jesus and transformed it into a glorious body, freed from the restrictions and limitations of the old creation and now bursting with life and possibility, so he will do something analogous with heaven and earth and everything in them.

The beginning of a more glorious story

In this renewal of all things, we get the sense that the new heaven and new earth are not merely the happy end of the story but the beginning of a more glorious story. What that story will be is largely left to our imagination, but there are mysterious hints that the nations and their treasures will have a place in the future which God is planning:

> And the city has no need of sun or moon to shine on it, for the glory of God gives it light, and its lamp is the Lamb. By its light will the nations walk, and the kings of the earth will bring their glory into it, and its gates will never be shut by day—and there will be no night there. They will bring into it the glory and the honour of the nations.
>
> *Revelation 21:23–26*

> Then the angel showed me the river of the water of life, bright as crystal, flowing from the throne of God and of the Lamb through the middle of the street of the city; also, on either side of the river, the tree of life with its twelve kinds of fruit, yielding its fruit each month. The leaves of the tree were for the healing of the nations.
>
> *Revelation 22:1–2*

Nothing of the life we live now will be wasted: whatever there is of value will be carried over into the new heaven and the new earth and will play its part in the great future story which, for the moment, is hidden in the heart and mind of God alone.

This full Christian hope, though it has often been misunderstood and reduced to something less than itself, has always been grasped and proclaimed by some of the followers of Jesus. Here, to conclude, are some words of the Scots preacher and writer George Macdonald (1824–1905) as he expounds Romans 8:

> When the sons of God show as they are, taking, with the character, the appearance and the place that belong to their sonship; when the sons of God sit with *the* Son of God on the throne of their

Father; then shall they be in potency of fact the lords of the lower creation, the bestowers of liberty and peace upon it; then shall the creation, subjected to vanity for their sakes, find its freedom in their freedom, its gladness in their sonship.[106]

For this the Son of God came, lived, died, and rose again. This is the Kingdom come in all its fullness.

Notes

1 Matthew 19:28.

2 Luke 20:47.

3 This assumes that the James who wrote the New Testament letter is the brother of Jesus: see Tom Wright, *Early Christian Letters for Everyone: James, Peter, John and Judah* (SPCK, 2014), p. 4.

4 Ernest Barker, *From Alexander to Constantine: Passages and Documents Illustrating the History of Social and Political Ideas 336 B.C.-A.D. 337* (Oxford University Press, 1956), p. 212. By permission of Oxford University Press.

5 Justin Welby, *Dethroning Mammon: Making Money Serve Grace* (Bloomsbury, 2016), p. 141.

6 Acts 28:31.

7 Romans 10:9, 1 Corinthians 12:3.

8 Hebrews 11:33.

9 Exodus 19:6.

10 1 Kings 21:3.

11 1 Kings 21:19.

12 Deuteronomy 15:4.

13 Genesis 2:15 (NIV).

14 See, for example, <http://www.huffingtonpost.com/armine-sahakyan/the-grim-pollution-pictur_b_9266764.html> (accessed 10 January 2017).

15 Luke 23:43.

16 The most recent revision of the *New International Version* reverts to the traditional (and more natural) translation of Paul's words: "*the* righteousness *of* God".

17 For a fuller explanation, see N. T. Wright, "Romans and the Theology of Paul" (1995), in Wright, *Pauline Perspectives: Essays on Paul, 1978–2013* (SPCK, 2013).

18 Genesis 12:3.

19 See Tom Wright, *Justification: God's Plan and Paul's Vision* (SPCK, 2009), pp. 132ff for a full discussion, on which the above is based.

20 See Wright, *Justification*, pp. 135ff for a full discussion, on which the above is based.

21 Romans 3:2.

22 There are other reasons it makes sense to opt for "faithfulness" rather than "faith": (1) the new translation avoids the redundancy of making Romans 3:22 read "through faith in Jesus Christ for the benefit of all who have faith"; (2) the new translation fits perfectly in the other contexts where the same or similar wording recurs: for instance, Romans 3:25f, Galatians 2:16, Galatians 2:20, Galatians 3:22.

23 See, for instance, J. I. Packer, "Justification" in *The Illustrated Bible Dictionary, Part 2* (Inter-Varsity Press, 1980), p. 843.

24 Galatians 2:17.

25 Philippians 3:9.

26 Galatians 2:17, as already quoted.

27 See John 4:9, 18:28.

28 Galatians 2:12.

29 Galatians 2:14.

30 Galatians 2:15.

31 Galatians 1:6.

32 1 John 3:8.

33 Some of this chapter is indebted to Tom Wright, *The Day the Revolution Began: Rethinking the Meaning of Jesus' Crucifixion* (SPCK, 2016).

34 Isaiah 53:6.

35 N. T. Wright, "The Letter to the Romans", in *The New Interpreter's Bible, Volume Ten* (Abingdon Press, 2002), p. 579. Copyright © 2002 Abingdon Press. Used by permission. All rights reserved.

36 Luke 9:31.

37 Matthew 27:24.

38 Romans 1:18.

39 See Robert Harris, *Selling Hitler: The Story of the Hitler Diaries* (Faber & Faber, 1986), pp. 16f for Hitler's vision of himself as an object of worship.

40 Galatians 4:9, 5:1.

41 <https://en.wikipedia.org/wiki/Jill_Saward> (accessed 18 January 2017).

[42]   Wright, *The Day the Revolution Began*, p. 75. Copyright © Tom Wright 2016. Reproduced with permission of the Licensor through PLSclear.

[43]   2 Chronicles 20:7, Isaiah 41:8.

[44]   Exodus 33:11.

[45]   Job 29:4.

[46]   John 16:8.

[47]   For a fuller account of Sister Lourdes' ministry, see Joseph D'souza & Benedict Rogers, *On the Side of the Angels: Justice, Human Rights, and Kingdom Mission* (Authentic, 2007), pp. 105ff.

[48]   John 1:46, 4:29.

[49]   See, for instance, Matthew 11:4, 13:16, Luke 7:22, 10:24, John 3:32, Acts 2:33, 4:20, 19:26, 22:15, 28:27.

[50]   Acts 10:38.

[51]   Matthew 28:17.

[52]   Matthew 6:30, 8:26, 14:31, 16:8, 17:20.

[53]   Luke 12:28.

[54]   Matthew 13:58.

[55]   Matthew 10:1, 10:8, Luke 9:2, 10:9.

[56]   See Bruce Collins, *Jesus' Gospel Jesus' Way* (Chilfrome Books, 2014), Book 2, pp. 81ff.

[57]   This is the approach of *The Book of Common Prayer*'s "Visitation of the Sick": God has sent your sickness, so make sure you learn the lessons he intends you to learn.

[58]   Dr & Mrs Howard Taylor, *Biography of James Hudson Taylor* (Hodder & Stoughton and OMF, 1973), pp. 347f.

[59]   Mark 9:24.

[60]   Matthew 5:48.

[61]   Parts of this chapter are indebted to the ideas in Tom Wright, *Virtue Reborn: The Transformation of the Christian Mind* (SPCK, 2010).

[62]   <https://en.wikipedia.org/wiki/The_7_Habits_of_Highly_Effective_People> (accessed 20 March 2017).

[63]   Romans 5:2.

[64]   Jeremiah 17:9.

[65]   Acts 2:37.

[66]   Galatians 6:8.

[67]   Colossians 3:5–12.

68 Matthew 6:1–18.

69 Daniel 9.

70 C. S. Lewis, *Miracles* (Collins/Fount Paperbacks, 1947), p. 167. MIRACLES by C. S. Lewis copyright © C. S. Lewis Pte. Ltd. 1947, 1960. Extract reprinted by permission.

71 Daniel 8:17.

72 1 Corinthians 13:10.

73 William F. Arndt and F. Wilbur Gingrich, *A Greek-English Lexicon of the New Testament* (University of Chicago Press, 1979), p. 57.

74 Jackie Pullinger, *Chasing the Dragon* (Hodder & Stoughton, 2001): see Chapter 5.

75 1 Corinthians 14:5.

76 See 1 Corinthians 12:30.

77 Taken from Wayne Grudem, *The Gift of Prophecy in the New Testament and Today* (Crossway, 1988, 2000), p. 51. Used by permission of Crossway, a publishing ministry of Good News Publishers, Wheaton, IL 60187, <www.crossway.org>.

78 Rosemarie Claussen, *Tears Turn to Diamonds* (Verlag Gottfried Bernard, 2010), p. 79.

79 <https://en.wikipedia.org/wiki/Word_of_Knowledge>, accessed 30 March 2018.

80 John 4:19.

81 Luke 7:39.

82 1 Corinthians 14:24–25.

83 Taken from Grudem, *The Gift of Prophecy*, p. 294. Used by permission of Crossway, a publishing ministry of Good News Publishers, Wheaton, IL 60187, <www.crossway.org>.

84 1 Corinthians 12:9—both words are plural.

85 1 Thessalonians 5:17.

86 Derek Kidner, *The Proverbs: An Introduction and Commentary* (Tyndale Press, 1969), p. 106. Some of the English versions miss the point of the proverb by substituting an "empty" manger for a "clean" one.

87 E.g. John Calvin, *The Gospel According to St John 1–10* (Eerdmans/Paternoster, 1995), p. 125.

88   James Packer, *Knowing God* (Hodder & Stoughton, 1973), pp. 54f. Copyright © 1973 by J. I. Packer. Reproduced by permission of Hodder and Stoughton Limited.

89   © 1961, Karl Barth, *Church Dogmatics—Volume IV: The Doctrine of Reconciliation* Part One (T. & T. Clark), p. 193.

90   Walter Hooper (ed.), *C. S. Lewis: Collected Letters—Volume II* (HarperCollins, 2004), p. 503. COLLECTED LETTERS VOL II by C. S. Lewis copyright © C. S. Lewis Pte. Ltd. 2004. Extract reprinted by permission.

91   C. S. Lewis, "Christianity and Literature" in *Christian Reflections* (Eerdmans, 2014), p. 8. CHRISTIAN REFLECTIONS by C. S. Lewis copyright © C. S. Lewis Pte. Ltd. 1967, 1980. Extract reprinted by permission.

92   Saint Augustine, tr. Edmund Hill, O.P., "The Trinity", in *The Works of Saint Augustine: A Translation for the 21st Century* (New City Press, 1991), pp. 98f.

93   Augustine, tr. Hill, "Homilies on the Gospel of John 1–40" in *The Works of Saint Augustine*, pp. 364f.

94   Augustine, tr. Hill, "Homilies", pp. 372f.

95   John 1:3 (NIV).

96   John 14:10.

97   See Kevin Giles, *Jesus and the Father: Modern Evangelicals Reinvent the Doctrine of the Trinity* (Zondervan, 2006), pp. 270f.

98   John 15:5.

99   Matthew 5:12.

100 Matthew 6:20.

101 Matthew 19:28.

102 Colossians 1:20.

103 Philippians 3:11.

104 Philippians 3:14 (my italics).

105 See Stephen Kuhrt, *Tom Wright for Everyone: Putting the Theology of N. T. Wright into Practice in the Local Church* (SPCK, 2011), p. 71.

106 George Macdonald, "Abba, Father!" in *The Unspoken Sermons*, Series Two. <http://www.online-literature.com/george-macdonald/unspoken-sermons/19/> (accessed 22 September 2018).

Lightning Source UK Ltd.
Milton Keynes UK
UKHW022026080720
366229UK00005B/170